More Praise for Tim Desmond

"This book shows us why self-compassion is at the heart of therapeutic healing, and how to integrate compassion training into clinical practice. A long time meditator and skilled clinician, Tim Desmond offers exceptionally clear, accessible, and insightful guidance in how to facilitate deep transformation while addressing a spectrum of emotional suffering."

—**Tara Brach, PhD,** author of *Radical Acceptance* and *True Refuge*

"This book is an extraordinarily practical and useful guide to the importance of self-compassion in psychotherapy. It is also a 'how-to' manual of simple practices that can be used to kindle the development of self-compassion. . . . [Desmond's] wonderful insights, vignettes, and wise teachings . . . will be of great benefit to any clinician who wishes to incorporate compassion practices in his or her work."

—**Richard J. Davidson, PhD,** Founder of the Center for Investigating Healthy Minds, University of Wisconsin-Madison

"Tim Desmond takes clinicians on a compelling journey to the heart of both mindfulness and psychotherapy. He offers clear principles and vivid examples for how to integrate self-compassion into relationship-based, individual therapy. A unique contribution is showing how at-home practices can emerge naturally from a mindful and compassionate co-exploration of the client's experience. Highly recommended for clinicians who wish to more deeply integrate mindfulness and psychotherapy."

—**Christopher Germer, PhD,** author of *The Mindful Path to Self-Compassion*

"Masterfully written, this book is a timely treasure trove of practical tools and exquisite examples of how to incorporate self-compassion practices into every moment of the therapeutic process. Tim Desmond expertly weaves together ancient teachings and modern insight into a clear, in-depth road map for the integration of two powerful paradigms of healing and transformation."

—**Linda Graham, MFT,** psychotherapist and author of *Bouncing Back: Rewiring Your Brain for Maximum Resilience and Well-Being*

"Vividly described vignettes from the author's therapeutic work with clients, and an excellent review of the research interweave in this book. The author is a gifted storyteller, and his writing is easy and compelling to read. . . . He brings each client to life with affection and insight, and offers a simple step-by-step process for therapists to use each vignette as a guide. . . . He shares original practices he has created, ancient Buddhist practices he has adapted, and practices created by modern teachers."

—The Mindfulness Bell

"Desmond describes mindfulness and self-compassion in a way that is useful for the neophyte or well informed. . . . [His] case studies wonderfully demonstrate not only a straightforward way of working with clients, but also how to work past the defenses the client uses to maintain their 'story.' . . . I highly recommend this book for practitioners at any level. The ideas apply across the board from client's to therapist's mental health and wellness." *—The Milton H. Erickson Foundation Newsletter*

"[I]n its integration of Buddhist philosophies with evidence-based scientific findings, this book offers a clear and heartfelt examination of the power of self-compassion in building the resilience needed to cope with suffering and achieve an enduring sense of happiness. Moreover, it comes as a much-needed, kind and gentle reminder for therapists to tend to their own emotional needs in order to provide improved service to their clients." *—Somatic Psychotherapy Today*

"This book is intended especially for clinicians, but can also be useful for researchers, teachers and students at all levels of expertise. I heartily recommend it both for clinicians who wish to build the capacity for self-compassion in their clients as well as themselves, and therefore more deeply integrate mindfulness and psychotherapy, and also as a valuable tool for classroom use to facilitate discussions for any classes in clinical psychology." *—Metapsychology Online Reviews*

"[S]elf-compassion and compassion toward others allows us to strategically empower our clients — and it also allows us to help ourselves cope with the stressors and duties of the profession. . . . [Desmond] does a good job of providing general tools that therapists can easily incorporate into their sessions." *—PsychCentral*

The
Self-Compassion
Skills

WORKBOOK

ALSO BY TIM DESMOND

Self-Compassion in Psychotherapy

The Self-Compassion Skills

WORKBOOK

A 14-Day Plan to Transform
Your Relationship with Yourself

Learn powerful, mindfulness-based techniques to help you:
— Motivate yourself with kindness instead of criticism
— Overcome negative emotions, depression, and anxiety
— Let go of self-criticism and self-sabotage
— Feel happier and more alive

TIM DESMOND

W.W. NORTON & COMPANY
Independent Publishers Since 1923
New York / London

Important Note: *The Self-Compassion Skills Workbook* is intended to provide general information on the subject of health and well-being; it is not a substitute for medical or psychological treatment and may not be relied upon for purposes of diagnosing or treating any illness. Please seek out the care of a professional healthcare provider if you are pregnant, nursing, or experiencing symptoms of any potentially serious condition.

For information about permission to reproduce selections from this book, write to Permissions, W. W. Norton & Company, Inc., 500 Fifth Avenue, New York, NY 10110

For information about special discounts for bulk purchases, please contact
W. W. Norton Special Sales at specialsales@wwnorton.com or 800-233-4830

Manufacturing by Edwards Brothers Malloy
Production manager: Christine Critelli

Library of Congress Cataloging-in-Publication Data

Names: Desmond, Tim, author.
Title: The self-compassion skills workbook : a 14-day plan to transform your
    relationship with yourself / Tim Desmond.
Description: First edition. I New York : W.W. Norton & Company, [2017] I
    Includes bibliographical references and index.
Identifiers: LCCN 2016035695 I ISBN 9780393712186 (pbk.)
Subjects: LCSH: Self-acceptance. I Compassion. I Meditation—Therapeutic use.
    I Mindfulness (Psychology)
Classification: LCC BF575.S37 D475 2017 I DDC 158.1—dc23 LC record
    available at https://lccn.loc.gov/2016035695

W. W. Norton & Company, Inc.
500 Fifth Avenue, New York, N.Y. 10110
www.wwnorton.com

W. W. Norton & Company Ltd.
15 Carlisle Street, London W1D 3BS

1 2 3 4 5 6 7 8 9 0

Contents

How to Use This Workbook

Just 14 days of self-compassion training can create significant and measurable changes in your brain, mind, and behavior. The practices contained in this workbook have been studied in rigorous, randomized, controlled trials (similar to the way a drug company tests a new medication), and scientists have concluded that as little as 30 minutes a day for 14 days is enough to create real and lasting change.[i]

Part I of this book is your preparation. It explains what self-compassion is, why it's so important, and illustrates what it looks like in various situations. This conceptual understanding of self-compassion gets you ready to begin your practical training.

Part II of this book is the program—your practical training in developing self-compassion. I suggest you set aside 30 minutes a day for 14 days for this purpose. At the end of that time, you will likely find that you feel more emotionally stable and comfortable with yourself. You'll find that joy comes more easily, and that your fears and anxieties pass more quickly. Once you've experienced the benefits of self-compassion training firsthand, you may decide to continue with your practice indefinitely.

If you can't manage 30 minutes a day, or if you can't commit to practicing every day for 14 days, *just do whatever you can.* Practicing for 5 minutes is much better than not practicing at all.

Each training session will be guided by the Map to Self-Compassion, which is explained in detail in Chapter 4. You begin each training session at the top of this map, and it will guide you to the most appropriate practice for you, depending on what you're feeling and how you respond to each exercise. The practice instructions for each exercise also point to corresponding audio tracks on "Guided Meditations for Self-Compassion", a downloadable companion resource available to readers at http://www.selfcompassionworkbook.com/.

As you're going through a particular exercise, it's perfectly normal for difficulties to arise. That is not a problem. Rather, that's the reason this workbook is organized the way it is. If you encounter any difficulty with a particular practice, jump to the end of that section and there will be specific guidance about what to do next.

We know that developing any new skill requires practice. If you want to play the piano, you have to invest some time and energy to learn. Just like a book on teaching yourself piano, this workbook requires actually practicing the exercises in Part II for you to receive most of the benefit. The more you practice (and the more consistently), the more benefit you'll receive. Practicing for 30 minutes a day for 14 days is a suggestion based on scientific research. However, if you can't commit 30 minutes, do what you can.

Part III is all about applying self-compassion to every part of your life. It is there to inspire you to use these methods to find greater health, peace, and happiness, as well as to benefit others.

I hope you find this workbook to be helpful in your life. Different practices are useful to different people at different times, so if something you read here doesn't fit for you, just let it go and move on. You might find the next practice more helpful. By the same token, a practice that feels stressful one day might feel liberating a few days later. If you bring your willingness to experiment, you will almost certainly find ways of using these practices that benefit you.

The
Self-Compassion
Skills

WORKBOOK

PART I

Introduction to Self-Compassion

What Is
Self-Compassion?

SELF-COMPASSION IS JUST WHAT IT SOUNDS LIKE. IT MEANS BEING COMPAS-sionate toward yourself. It means celebrating and enjoying yourself when life is going well, as well as being kind and forgiving toward yourself when life is hard.

So much of our pain comes from criticizing ourselves and other people. We feel cut off from others, ashamed and alone. Maybe we can point to some specific terrible thing that happened to us, or maybe we've felt anxious and depressed for as long as we can remember. We might believe that life is supposed to be different than it is, or that we won't be lovable until we get rid of whatever we think is wrong with us.

On the other hand, it's possible to feel loved, accepted, and appreciated for being exactly who we are. We can know—deep down in our bones—that we are fundamentally OK—and even more than OK. Somewhere inside of us there is a wise voice that knows we are beautiful and unique human beings. We can learn to hear that voice and believe it.

This is exactly what I mean by self-compassion. Self-compassion is the recognition that no matter what is happening in our lives, we are lovable. When things are going well, self-compassion gives us the permission to feel joy. When we're suffering or experiencing any kind of distress, self-compassion becomes a kind and supportive voice within that helps us find beauty and meaning.

Self-Compassion in My Life

I grew up in and around Boston with a single, alcoholic mother. We were always struggling financially and were even homeless for a summer when I

3

was a teenager. By the time I got to college, I was carrying around a tremendous amount of anger, sadness, and loneliness.

It was in college that I was introduced to the practice of self-compassion, through the Vietnamese Buddhist teacher Thich Nhat Hanh. I immediately recognized that it had been exactly what was missing from my life. As I immersed myself in these practices, I began to experience more peace, joy, and freedom than I had ever thought possible.

Self-compassion has completely transformed my life. From someone with an intense amount of suffering and self-destructiveness, I have become someone who today knows a lot of peace and enjoys a great deal of harmony and intimacy in my relationships.

But how does that work? It's not like self-compassion is a magic shield that protects us from bad things happening, or from ever having to feel sad. Self-compassion allows us to take good care of ourselves when we are faced with life's inevitable difficulties. Anxiety, frustration, and loneliness will still arise, but self-compassion helps us not to get stuck in them. We can embrace our own suffering like a mother holding a newborn baby, and soon begin to feel better.

In my life I've learned that true inner peace and freedom come from being able to love and accept myself regardless of what's going on. I know—from scientific research and from my own experience—that no matter how much pain and negativity I might be carrying around in myself, it is possible to develop self-compassion. This workbook contains all the building blocks you need to begin.

I decided to become a therapist because I wanted to share what has been so helpful in my life with others, especially people experiencing emotional pain. I hope that you will benefit from these practices as much as I have.

Self-Compassion When Life Is Going Well and When It Feels Hard

The following exercises will help you to recognize the difference between self-compassion and other types of attitudes.

When life is going well . . .	
As you read the following statements, notice which resonate with you and circle them. These are attitudes that can arise when life is going well.	
Self-critical attitude (examples)	**Self-compassionate attitude (examples)**
• I don't deserve this.	• I deserve good things, just like everyone else.
• This means something bad is going to happen soon.	• I don't know what the future holds, but I'm glad this is happening now.
• People are going to discover I'm a phony.	• If people really understood me, they'd like me.
• People will hate me if they see me happy.	• If people are jealous of me, it's because they haven't learned how to recognize what's beautiful in their own lives.

When life is going well, self-compassion allows us to enjoy it without feeling guilty. We know that we deserve good things in life—not because we are better than other people, but just because we are human beings. Compassion isn't something we have to earn. It comes from the recognition that everyone is born with basic human worth.

When life feels hard . . .	
As you read the following statements, notice which ones resonate with you and circle them. These are attitudes that can arise when life feels hard.	
Self-critical attitude (examples)	**Self-compassionate attitude (examples)**
• I deserve to suffer.	• I know that everyone suffers sometimes. When we suffer, we need love and support.
• This is happening because I'm a loser (or a bad person, etc.).	• When life is challenging, I can use it to learn and grow.
• If I weren't so stupid and incompetent, I wouldn't have to deal with this.	• Every human being experiences suffering, no matter how many virtues they have.

• My entire life is pain and disappointment.	⊙ No matter what I do, difficult things will happen in life. However, there are also many beautiful things in life that I don't want to ignore.

Self-compassion is particularly important when we're dealing with challenges in life. When we're really struggling—feeling afraid, depressed, angry, or lonely—what we need most is understanding and love. The problem is that we can't always rely on other people to be there when we need them. And even if we have a great support system, many of us find it difficult to open ourselves up to love from others.

However, if we can develop a source of deep understanding and compassion within ourselves, it is always there when we need it. It becomes the foundation for greater strength, resilience, and peace of mind. And fortunately, this is possible for anyone who is willing to practice.

SELF-COMPASSION STORY: JARED ISN'T ALONE

Jared had dealt with loneliness from a very young age. He had always struggled to make friends and felt that he was different from all the other kids at school.

However, his life improved considerably as an adult. His coworkers generally seemed to like him, and he was in a committed relationship with a kind woman. Despite this, he still suffered from bouts of overwhelming loneliness that bordered on clinical depression. He felt like an imposter and was afraid that everyone would see through his act and reject him.

Jared learned about self-compassion at a meditation retreat through the following exercise. He put his hand on his heart and told himself, "It makes sense that you feel lonely. You were alone for such a big part of your life. But that wasn't your fault. You were born into a bad situation and didn't get the support you needed. You've always been lovable, and the people in your adult life can see that."

He experienced this practice as deeply healing and began to use it nearly every day. He found that whenever his loneliness would start to emerge, 15 minutes of self-compassion was enough to help him regain balance.

How Is Self-Compassion Different From Self-Esteem?

We all know that *low self-esteem* is a bad thing. It is correlated with pretty much every kind of mental health problem. But not everyone knows that *high self-esteem* can be a problem as well.

Self-esteem means judging or evaluating yourself positively. You believe that you are a good person, and you identify with your strengths. However, research has shown that for most of us, believing we are good is closely related to believing we are better than other people.

This is the main problem with being overly focused on self-esteem. If I need to believe that I'm better than other people in order to have high self-esteem, it can make me more likely to criticize others, and more fearful of people seeing my weaknesses. I can become too competitive, and too fragile when receiving negative feedback.

On the other hand, when you have self-compassion you don't care if you are better, worse, or the same as anyone else. Self-compassion just means relating to yourself with a kind and forgiving attitude no matter what is happening.

When we relate to ourselves with self-compassion, there is no need to put other people down. We aren't afraid of occasional failures because we can see them as valuable learning opportunities instead of threats to our self-worth. In fact, researchers have found that self-compassion actually improves our motivation to succeed because we aren't so worried about making mistakes. We don't need to be perfect in order to be lovable.

SELF-COMPASSION STORY: LETTING GO OF PERFECTIONISM

Karen is a journalist who works at one of the top newspapers in the country. She is intelligent and hardworking, but rarely smiles. Karen admitted to her therapist that she often feels deeply insecure and empty inside. She works 80 hours a week or more, and explained that whenever she takes time off from work, she starts to feel depressed.

Karen's therapist decided to work with her on developing more self-compassion. She asked Karen to talk about a recent disappointment in her life, and Karen replied that she had felt bad when her editor emailed her yesterday asking if she had any new stories that she was ready to submit. She didn't, and described feeling a lot of panic. Her self-talk sounded like, "What is wrong with you? Are you losing it? Just write a story and make it good! Stop being a baby!" Karen's face was full of tension as she recounted the ordeal.

Karen's therapist guided her through the Map to Self-Compassion (Part II of this book), during which Karen realized that she was using this self-criticism to motivate herself to succeed. However, it had become so strong that it was now overwhelming to her. She pictured herself reading the email from her editor and tried saying to herself, "Dear Karen, I know you're scared of failing, and that's OK. Everyone gets scared sometimes. I also know you want to write great stories, and that is wonderful. You should write a great story because you want to, not because you're afraid that you'll be worthless if you don't. I love you no matter what."

It took some time, but Karen started internalizing this kind of self-talk and she found that she was more productive than ever, especially because now she could relax.

Is Self-Compassion Ever Bad?

The short answer is *no*.

The longer answer is that many people think they are practicing self-compassion when they are actually engaging in something quite different. Although true self-compassion is always helpful, there are some imposters that can be harmful. Here are a few of those imposters:

— **Self-indulgence:** The term *self-indulgence*, which is defined in the dictionary as "excessive or unrestrained gratification of one's own appetites, desires, or whims," suggests an unwillingness to invest effort to make meaningful changes in yourself or the world. Retreating from the world and putting forth no effort to improve yourself and your circumstances is actually incompatible with true self-compassion. Even though self-compassion means understanding that you are perfectly lovable just as you are right now, you still value enhancing your life through growth. When you have self-compassion, you don't *need to change*, but you *like to grow*. Growth often requires exerting effort (although it also involves allowing yourself to rest and *just be* when that's what you need most). In contrast, self-indulgence implies the mistaken belief that admitting you have more to learn in life somehow means that you aren't acceptable the way you are. Self-compassion, however, includes an understanding that we always have more to learn, and that learning and growth are fundamental parts of life.

— **Self-pity:** *Self-pity* is defined as "excessive, self-absorbed unhappiness over one's own troubles." It implies the belief that you are weak and incapable of improving your situation. The term *self-pity* suggests that life is something that *happens to you*, that you are a victim of circumstances and have no role in shaping your experience. This is not the same as self-compassion. With self-compassion, you are aware that you're capable of doing great things. Like everyone, you have strengths and weaknesses, and you can develop new strengths if you want to. You don't have to be strong in every way in order to be lovable, but part of loving yourself is seeing what you are capable of.

— **Passivity:** Compassion naturally leads to action. If we see that our baby is hungry, we don't just empathize with her hunger. We take action and feed her. Although self-compassion sometimes involves just a change in attitude, real compassion includes the desire to relieve suffering, either for ourselves or someone else, and might require that we make a concrete change to some aspect of our lives.

- **Egotism:** Viewing yourself as better than another person or being overly involved with your own needs at the expense of another's is not practicing self-compassion. As mentioned earlier, when you practice self-compassion you are not concerned with comparing yourself to others; you value everyone's happiness. This certainly doesn't mean that you are being egotistical when you value or prioritize your own needs. It means that true self-compassion enhances your compassion for others rather than undermining it.

SELF-COMPASSION STORY: HEALING TRAUMA

Jennifer was driving on the highway when the car next to her tried to change lanes and crashed into her. Her car then slammed into the guardrail and was totaled. Luckily, she sustained only mild injuries and was physically healthy within a month. However, more than a year later, Jennifer was still experiencing symptoms of posttraumatic stress. She avoided driving whenever she could, and when she had to drive, she was overwhelmed with anxiety.

She began working with a therapist who was familiar with the Map to Self-Compassion, and he guided Jennifer to visualize someone who could completely love and accept her. Jennifer chose her grandmother (who had been deceased for several years), and imagined her grandmother saying, "May you be happy. May you be healthy. May you be safe. May you be loved." After imagining this for just a few minutes, Jennifer reported feeling more peaceful than she had in a long time. She began using this practice whenever she had to drive or felt anxious in any way, and after a few months she was able to drive again with confidence.

The Promise of Self-Compassion

Whatever challenges you are facing in life—whether it's trauma, relationship problems, self-criticism, or anxiety—self-compassion can help. It is like having a loving and supportive friend who is always with you—someone who can listen, understand, and help you find a new perspective. It gives you an internal source of emotional regulation and resilience, and it helps you to be more fully present with what is beautiful in life.

Self-Compassion Is a Skill

THE FIRST STEP IN DEVELOPING ANY NEW SKILL IS FEELING CONFIDENT THAT you are capable of doing it. Fortunately, every scientist who has studied the development of compassion and self-compassion has concluded that it is possible for *anyone* to develop self-compassion. No matter how self-critical or angry or hopeless you feel, it is possible for *you*.

The second step in developing a new skill is being motivated enough to work at it. One of the most important factors in cultivating self-compassion is your willingness to practice. If you want to learn how to speak a new language or play a musical instrument, everyone knows that practice is necessary. It's the same with developing self-compassion. If you are willing to dedicate yourself to practicing the Map to Self-Compassion (Part II of this workbook) and invest your time and energy, I promise that you will experience real benefits.

Can I Really Become Self-Compassionate?			
Read the statement in the left column (The fear) and rate how much it resonates for you, from 0 to 10. Then read the statement in the right column (The reality) 3 times, pausing to take a breath each time. Finally, rate how true the second statement seems, from 0 to 10. This exercise is designed to help strengthen the confidence you feel in your ability to develop self-compassion.			
The fear:	**0–10**	**The reality:**	**0–10**
"This is just how I am. It's too late for me to change."	3	People can learn new skills and develop new strengths throughout their lives.	10
"I have a chemical imbalance. There is nothing I can do about it."	5	Science has proven that compassion training can change the chemistry of our brains.	7
"I've tried everything, and nothing can help me."	1	We might have tried many things, but not everything.	10
"I don't deserve compassion."	0	We absolutely *do* deserve compassion, simply because we are human beings.	9

Self-Compassion and Your Brain

Dr. Richard Davidson, one of the leading neuroscientists in the world, has studied how compassion training affects your brain. He's concluded that anyone can develop greater compassion and self-compassion, but that it requires practice. If you practice a little, you can develop a little self-compassion. If you practice a lot, you can develop a lot.

According to Davidson's research, there is no limit to the amount of compassion and self-compassion that we can develop if we dedicate ourselves to practice. In fact, when he studied Buddhist monks who had undergone decades of intensive compassion training, he reported that they had developed a level of inner peace and freedom beyond what most people would believe possible. In other words, the sky is the limit. If you are willing to train yourself in the practices that make up the Map to Self-Compassion, you can transform your life.

All humans (in fact, all mammals) have a Care Circuit in their brain. Every time you feel warmth and love, that brain circuit is active. If we could take a detailed image of your brain, you would see it. Your Care Circuit releases oxytocin (sometimes called the love hormone) and natural opiates to give you that warm fuzzy feeling.

As you begin training in self-compassion, your Care Circuit is going to be your best friend. You'll be learning different practices that can activate it, strengthen it, use it for emotional regulation, and to become kinder toward yourself.

Developing self-compassion is relatively simple. It is about strengthening the Care Circuit in your brain and learning how to use it when you need it.

EIGHT SCIENTIFIC DISCOVERIES ABOUT SELF-COMPASSION

1. There is a specific circuit in your brain that scientists call the *Care Circuit*, which creates the experience of compassion, warmth, and love.[ii]

2. Self-compassion training strengthens your Care Circuit—like exercising a muscle.[iii]

3. With enough compassion training, your Care Circuit can literally grow in size so that the increase is visible on a brain scan. [iv]

4. The Care Circuit is one of the primary emotional circuits in the brain that creates happiness and well-being.[v]

5. Activating the Care Circuit through self-compassion training reduces every form of emotional distress, including anxiety, depression, and anger.[vi]

6. Compassion training for *30 minutes a day for 14 days* creates significant changes in the brain and leads to more prosocial and altruistic behavior.[vii]

7. *Eight weeks* of compassion training can make your temperament or personality significantly more positive.[viii]

8. Scientists have documented that Buddhist monks with intensive training in compassion have the *strongest markers for happiness* in their brains that have ever been recorded.[ix]

SELF-COMPASSION STORY: THIS IS WHAT 20 YEARS OF PRACTICE LOOKS LIKE

Margaret grew up in a poor coal-mining town in West Virginia in the 1950s. It was a rough place to be a kid and she learned how to fight, both verbally and physically, before she could ride a bike.

Her hot temper and love for arguing helped her in college, where she was on the debate team. However, they also meant she had a hard time making close friends. She would verbally attack anyone at the slightest hint of a disagreement.

In her late 20s, Margaret began exploring meditation as a way to calm her temper. Her teacher helped her see how scared she felt during the split second before she verbally attacked someone. He recommended that she try sending herself compassion as soon as that fear came up.

This practice was revolutionary for her. It made her feel so much better that she started worrying if she was using it too much. When she asked her teacher if there was such a thing as too much self-compassion, he said "no," so she began sending herself love and compassion from the time she woke up until she went to bed. As she was eating, driving, or working, she would be silently saying to herself, "May you be happy. May you have ease. May you be free. May you be loved."

Twenty years later, Margaret is a highly respected meditation teacher in her own right. Her temper is gone, and her students describe her as one of the most loving and caring people in the world.

There is no limit to the amount of compassion (for yourself and others) that you can develop in your life if you are willing to practice. Your body and your brain are designed to feel compassion, and the more you engage your Care Circuit, the stronger and bigger it becomes. There is nothing stopping you from developing a radically new way of relating to yourself—with kindness and love.

What Self-Compassion Looks Like: Vignettes and Exercises

IN THIS CHAPTER, YOU'LL SEE WHAT SELF-COMPASSION LOOKS LIKE IN vignettes—short descriptive stories that illustrate issues related to self-compassion—and you'll also find exercises to help you learn about your own attitudes that affect self-compassion. When you have a clear understanding of exactly what self-compassion means, you'll be ready to begin the 14-day training program in Part II of this workbook.

Motivating Yourself With Kindness

Many people are afraid that if they stop criticizing themselves, they will no longer be motivated to grow and succeed. However, research has shown that the exact opposite is true. People who motivate themselves with kindness (rather than criticism) are much better at persevering through adversity and using failures as opportunities to learn.[x]

SELF-COMPASSION STORY: MARCUS'S EXAMS

Marcus is a first-year student in law school who is getting ready for final exams. He's wanted to be a lawyer since he was 10 years old, so this is a dream come true for him. Marcus has always done well on tests, but the amount of material he's expected to know for these exams is much larger than ever before.

Marcus could relate to this situation in several different ways. Notice the difference between a self-critical and a self-compassionate response to his exams.

SELF-CRITICAL RESPONSE

Marcus thinks to himself, "Don't blow it. You've wanted this your whole life, so you better not screw it up now. Don't be a loser. Don't be a baby. Don't be an idiot. You've got to learn everything, because you can be sure that the one thing you skip is going to be on the test and you will flunk. If you flunk, your life is over! Flunking this test means you will never get a job and you will be a complete failure. Now get going and study! No excuses!

How much of the time do you think like this? (0–100%) _30%_

SELF-COMPASSIONATE RESPONSE

Marcus thinks to himself, "You're afraid of failing at this, and that's OK. You really want to succeed as a lawyer and this is important to you. It makes sense you'd be scared. But no matter what happens, you'll be OK. If you end up being a lawyer, that will be wonderful. If not, you will find something else that you love. Regardless of what happens, you will learn and grow from this experience. I know you are capable of passing these exams if you give it your full effort. I know you can do it. I believe in you.

How much of the time do you think like this? (0–100%) _50%_

A comparison of these two possible reactions might suggest that Marcus would *feel better* using self-compassion, but that he might *study harder* using self-criticism. However, research shows that this isn't necessarily true.[xi]

More importantly, Marcus will eventually have to face some setback or misfortune. Motivating ourselves with criticism is all about making ourselves fear failure, which often results in our avoiding challenges that might result in failure. We shrink from our setbacks and challenges because we're afraid of our inner-critic.

I see this situation every day working with talented, intelligent people whose self-criticism has become paralyzing. They become so afraid of angering that violent self-critical voice that they refuse to do anything that could trigger it. They stop attempting anything that they could fail, and eventually become afraid to admit they want to do something new. For example, "I can't let myself *want* that promotion, because If I don't get it, my inner-critic will destroy me."

On the other hand, if Marcus uses self-compassion, it is going to be a much better strategy over the long term, especially when he has to deal with life's inevitable difficulties. People like Steve Jobs and Michael Jordan are famous for talking about how many times they've failed in their lives. In fact, there is a famous quote in which Jordan describes all the times he was trusted to take a game-winning shot and missed. He says his willingness to fail is why he has succeeded. Self-compassion allows us to keep taking risks and doing things that we aren't certain will succeed, which means we can keep learning and growing. In fact, there is substantial research that shows people with high levels of self-compassion can achieve more because they are better able to persevere through difficulties.[xii]

For Marcus, part of motivating himself with kindness was recognizing that his worth doesn't come from succeeding in school. Whether he succeeds or not, he can still feel OK. It is an attitude that says, "Do this because you want to, not because it's the only way for you to have any worth as a human being."

EXERCISE: MARISHA'S FIRST MARATHON

Marisha is attempting her first marathon. She's had plenty of training, so she knows she's prepared. However, about two thirds into her race, her legs seem heavier than they ever have before. She really hopes to finish.

How can she motivate herself?

In this exercise you'll write two different ways Marisha could try to motivate herself. One will use self-criticism, and the other will use self-compassion. This will help you to get clearer about how they are different.

SELF-CRITICAL RESPONSE

(Write what she might think to motivate herself with self-criticism. For example, "Don't be weak!")

"You have been training so long for this how can you be tired now? You're not even close to finished yet, c'mon don't be a baby and don't be weak. If you don't finish all that training would have been for nothing"

SELF-COMPASSIONATE RESPONSE

(Write what she might think to motivate herself with self-compassion. Make sure that she accepts that she's struggling and encourages herself with kindness. For example, "I know this is hard, but you'll make it through.")

"You're legs may be tired but I know you can do this. You are so strong and you are capable of such great things. You're almost there and you'll make it to that finish line, you got this."

Self-Compassion When Life Is Hard

The times in our lives when we most need compassion are moments of loss, rejection, failure, and other misfortunes. The problem is that we don't always have a kind and caring person available at those times to offer emotional support. However, when we have developed self-compassion, this care and support is present inside ourselves whenever we need it most.

We all have pain from our past that we carry around with us—moments in which we felt entirely cut off from love and compassion. In fact, we could even define *emotional pain* as the *absence of compassion*. It is especially important, therefore, that we develop *self-compassion*—the ability to generate compassion for ourselves—so that we will never be completely without this vital energy. Practicing self-compassion in life's challenging moments provides us with a deep source of resilience and strength.

SELF-COMPASSION STORY: JACK'S DATE

Jack went on a first date with a woman he really liked. She was smart and funny, and Jack thought they got along really well. However, when he called her to ask for a second date, she didn't even answer. A few hours later he received a text that said, "You're a great guy, but I don't think we're a good match. Sorry."

Let's look at how Jack could be critical of himself, critical of the woman, or respond with compassion.

SELF-CRITICAL RESPONSE

Jack thinks, "Of course she doesn't like me. Why would she? She's too good for me. I must have said something stupid or she just thinks I'm ugly. Why am I so lame and weird looking? I wish I were a different person. I hate who I am."

How much of the time do you think like this? (0–100%) __40%__

OTHER-CRITICAL RESPONSE

Jack thinks, "Are you kidding me? Who does she think she is? There is something seriously wrong with her. I bet she's the type of woman who only likes alcoholics or stupid guys so she can feel superior. I hope she dies alone."

How much of the time do you think like this? (0–100%) _5_ %.

SELF-COMPASSIONATE RESPONSE

Jack thinks, "I'm disappointed and sad. I was really hoping to get to know her better. It's OK to let myself feel sad when something I want doesn't happen. I don't need to make these feelings go away." James puts his hands on his heart and pays attention to the sensation of his breath as it goes in and out. He gives himself some time to feel his feelings. When his sadness begins to lessen, he thinks, "This didn't work out, but there's no way to know if dating her would have been wonderful or terrible. It's possible that this is going to open me up for something much better. I wanted to date her, but sometimes life has even better plans for us."

How much of the time do you think like this? (0–100%) _30_ %.

Looking at Jack's self-compassionate response, a few things stand out.

— He named his feelings. Rather than looking to blame anyone, he recognized he was feeling sad and disappointed.

— He gave himself time and space to feel his feelings without trying to make them go away. This is a form of self-acceptance (see Practice 2: Self-Acceptance, to learn ways of creating this kind of space more deliberately in your own life).

— Finally, he used some positive and encouraging thinking to reframe his experience into something more hopeful. However, he waited until he had spent some time just accepting and allowing his feelings before trying to change his thinking.

SELF-COMPASSION EXERCISE: SASHA'S CAR

Sasha parked her car in the parking lot of a shopping mall. When she returned an hour later, there was a huge dent in her rear passenger door. She looked for a note, but there wasn't one. Someone had hit her car and left.

How could Sasha respond?

SELF-PITY RESPONSE

(Write what she might think if she responds with self-pity. She doesn't blame herself, but she feels like a helpless victim. For example, "Why does this always happen to me? I must be cursed!")

"Of course this ~~would~~ would happen to me, things like this always happen to me. Anything that can go wrong, right? There is no note, how am I going to even handle this? I just have to accept that I'm cursed and that things like this will always continue!

SELF-CRITICAL RESPONSE

(Write what she might think if she responds with self-criticism. For example, "I'm so stupid! I should have noticed the other car was parked too close.")

"I should have checked the other side of my car, I was probably way too close, why do I always screw up. Why can't I do something right for once. I am so stupid. I wish I wasn't like this, if only I was more observant."

SELF-COMPASSIONATE RESPONSE

(Write what she might think if she responds with self-compassion. For example, "It's OK to feel sad about this. Whatever you feel is just fine. Remember, you are safe and there are a lot of wonderful things in life, too.")

"This is very upsetting and I understand that. You are allowed to feel upset. Just know that it will work out. You are so loved and appreciated and you have many wonderful things in your life."

Erasing Shame: Self-Compassion for the Past

We all carry around pain from the past within ourselves. Some call it emotional baggage or unresolved issues. My teacher, Thich Nhat Hanh, calls it the seeds of suffering that have been planted in the garden of our minds.

In my experience, self-compassion can be a tremendously powerful practice for healing pain from the past so that it will no longer burden us in the present.

SELF-COMPASSION STORY: CHERYL'S DIVORCE

Cheryl has been divorced for a little over 4 years, but every time she thinks about her divorce, she is filled with shame and self-loathing. She was married for 8 years, and over the course of that time, she and her husband developed powerful resentments toward each other. What began as inability to communicate about small conflicts eventually grew into bitterness and isolation. Her husband finally asked for a divorce, and she agreed because it was clear they were making each other miserable.

Now she dates occasionally, but she knows that unresolved pain from her divorce is preventing her from feeling safe and comfortable in a new relationship. She wants to heal this pain and begin anew.

Let's look at how Cheryl could blame herself, blame her husband, feel self-pity, or use self-compassion to heal.

SELF-CRITICAL RESPONSE

Cheryl could think, "I must be toxic. I ruined a perfectly good marriage because I can't communicate. There is something deeply wrong with me. I'm sure I will destroy any new relationship too. The best thing for me is to be alone so I won't ruin another man's life."

How much of the time do you think like this? (0–100%) _40%_

OTHER-CRITICAL RESPONSE

Cheryl could think, "This is all *his* fault. I can't believe he would do this to me. He destroyed our marriage and has made me hate myself. He is so negative and judgmental. I just hate him!"

How much of the time do you think like this? (0–100%) _20%_

SELF-PITY RESPONSE

Cheryl could think, "Why did this happen to me? Don't I deserve to be happy? What did I possibly do to deserve this life? Other people have good marriages and happy families, but not me. My life is ruined, and I'll never be happy again!"

How much of the time do you think like this? (0–100%) _40%._

SELF-COMPASSIONATE RESPONSE

Cheryl could think, "I need to give myself permission to grieve this loss without worrying about who is to blame. I don't really understand what went wrong, but I know that my marriage was incredibly painful. I also know that I felt completely starved of love and compassion." Cheryl takes all the time she needs to feel her sadness as sensations in her body *without getting caught in her stories about it*. Then she visualizes herself near the end of her marriage and sees how alone and unloved she felt. Picturing herself in the past, she says, "I know you feel so unloved right now, but I love you, and I see how special and lovable you are." She sends love and compassion to herself in the past, right in the moment that she needed it most. After continuing this practice each day for a few weeks, she discovers that she's not so afraid of a new relationship.

How much of the time do you think like this? (0–100%) _30%._ *This sounds wonderful + like such a healthy way to think*

For Cheryl, self-compassion meant accepting her feelings without getting lost in them. She gave herself permission to feel her grief as sensation in the body (Practice 2: Self-Acceptance), which kept her from being carried away by her stories and judgments. Then she used a visualization practice (see Practice 4: Healing Pain From the Past) to actively send herself compassion. She pictured herself during a moment that she felt completely cut off from love and compassion, near the end of her marriage. Then she visualized expressing compassion to herself in the past, saying "I know you feel so unloved right now, but I love you and I see how special and lovable you are."

SELF-COMPASSION EXERCISE: ANNA'S DIET

Anna has been overweight for most of her life. She always believed she could lose weight if she wanted to, but it wasn't important to her. If other people judged her because of her appearance, that was *their problem*. However, a year ago Anna's doctor told her that she was at risk for a heart attack and she needed to lose at least 30 pounds. Dieting and exercise proved much harder than Anna had thought they would. After 2 months with minimal results, she gave up trying to lose weight and found a different doctor.

Since that time, Anna has felt a great deal of shame about her weight. Whenever she eats or sees herself in the mirror, her inner-critic calls her weak and pathetic. She's afraid to try dieting again because failing was so painful.

Anna wants to heal this experience from her past. She begins by visualizing herself on the day she chose to give up her diet.

What could she say?

SELF-PITY RESPONSE

(Write what she might say if she responds with self-pity. Remember that a self-pity response acknowledges suffering, but assumes that you don't have the power to make things better. For example, "It's not your fault that you look like this. You have bad luck and there's nothing you can do about it.")

"You may be over weight but that is not your fault. That's just your genetics and not your fault, you have no control of it, youve just very unlucky and why should you have to work harder to be thin".

SELF-CRITICAL RESPONSE

(Write what she might say if she responds with self-criticism. For example, "You're so weak and pathetic.")

"I can't believe that you would give up so easy and then go out of your way to get a new doctor. You are absolutely pathetic and lazy and you are so unworthy of love.

SELF-COMPASSIONATE RESPONSE

(Write what she might say if she responds with self-compassion. For example, "I know it's scary and hard to do this. Whatever you're feeling is OK. It's alright if you need to take a break from your diet. You can just try again when you're ready. I want you to be healthy, but I don't want you to feel ashamed. No matter what, you are a lovable person.")

"The beginning will be tough and that's okay. I know that you will be able to do it if you set your mind to it. Don't get so hard on youself if you don't get it right away though because you are doing this for your wellbeing and it's okay if you need some time."

Compassion for Every Part of Ourselves

We all have parts of ourselves that we wish were different. We might wish our depression would go away, or our clumsiness, or our quick temper. However, this desire to grow and improve can become harmful if it turns into hating aspects of ourselves. There's a difference between wanting to worry less and hating myself when I worry. One is motivated by the desire to grow and the other is motivated by the belief that I am unacceptable as I am.

The deepest meaning of self-compassion is relating to *every part of ourselves* with compassion. We have compassion for our anxiety, for our loneliness, and even for our self-criticism. It means that every thought, every feeling, and every behavior can be embraced with compassion. In fact, when we learn how to have compassion for the parts of ourselves that give us the most discomfort and pain, we discover that growth and healing become much easier.

SELF-COMPASSION STORY: NANCY'S ANXIETY

Nancy is an editor and mom in her 40s who struggles with powerful anxiety. She's seen several therapists over the years and read dozens of self-help books, most of which have helped a little—but her anxiety continues to remain a problem.

Regardless of whether good things or bad things are happening in her life, Nancy worries. No matter how hard she tries, she hasn't been able to stop herself from thinking about every conceivable bad thing that could happen to her or her family.

Let's look at how Nancy could relate to her anxiety with either self-criticism or self-compassion.

SELF-CRITICAL RESPONSE

Nancy could think, "What's wrong with me? I'm doing it again and it's ruining my life. I hate it when I do this. *Stop worrying!* You're pathetic and weak. Just stop it."

How much of the time do you think like this? (0–100%) _50 %_

SELF-COMPASSIONATE RESPONSE

Nancy could think, "I'm worrying again, and I really wish I could stop." She sits down, puts her hands on her heart, and focuses on the physical tension and agitation in her body—giving herself permission to feel it without trying to change it. Then she visualizes her grandmother and thinks about how her grandmother can love and accept her even when she is overcome with worry. She imagines her grandmother saying, "No matter what you're feeling or what you're thinking, I love you completely." With just a few minutes of this practice, she feels much calmer.

How much of the time do you think like this? (0–100%) _0%_

It's easy to empathize with Nancy's self-critical response. She has a powerful desire to stop worrying so much because she sees that it's hurting her family and herself. The problem is that beating herself up hasn't helped.

Luckily, Nancy finds that self-compassion is much more effective for her. She begins by allowing herself to feel her feelings as sensations in her body (Practice 2: Self-Acceptance). By focusing on her body, she's able to avoid getting caught by the scary stories she's telling herself. She doesn't need to make those thoughts go away, and she doesn't need to fight against herself at all. She just needs to give herself permission to feel exactly what she's feeling already.

After a few minutes of that practice, Nancy shifts into a visualization (Practice 3: Embracing Suffering). She imagines her grandmother sending her love and compassion—not only to the parts of her that are strong, but also to her fear and pain. This is an example of embracing our suffering with compassion.

SELF-COMPASSION EXERCISE: JERRY'S ANGER

Jerry is in his late 20s and works for an online marketing company. In the past couple of years, he has come to realize that his anger is hurting his relationships and his quality of life. He loses his temper with clients, coworkers, and friends. His tendency to be judgmental has also ruined his last two romantic relationships.

Jerry really wants to control his temper, but his attempts so far haven't been very effective. How can Jerry deal with his anger?

SELF-CRITICAL RESPONSE

(Write what a self-critical way of relating to his anger might sound like. For example, "What's wrong with you? Stop being such a terrible person!")

"You're ruining everything! Why can't you just keep your mouth shut! You know that this is what is making you such a terrible person!

SELF-COMPASSIONATE RESPONSE

(Write what a self-compassionate way of relating to his anger might sound like. For example, "When you get angry, I know that it's because you're suffering, and you need compassion. It's OK for suffering to come up for you. Just remember to send yourself compassion.")

"I understand that you use anger as a way to deal with the pain that you are feeling, but it's okay to acknowledge that you just need to give yourself some compassion. I love you and think that you are a great person capable of many things."

PART II

The Map to Self-Compassion

Step-by-Step Guided Training Sessions

Navigating
the Map
Finding the Right Practice for You

"Well-being can be learned but it requires practice.
There is no substitute for practice."

— RICHARD DAVIDSON, PHD

RESEARCH SHOWS THAT ANYONE CAN DEVELOP SELF-COMPASSION. ALL THAT is required is a willingness to practice. The Map to Self-Compassion will guide you through experiential training sessions that have been shown to improve your ability to regulate intense emotions, be more resilient during life's challenges, let go of self-criticism or self-sabotage, and heal the pain from your past.

If you devote 30 minutes a day for 14 days to this form of training, you will see significant (and often life-changing) results.

The Map to Self-Compassion is an invaluable resource because it works like an experienced mentor guiding you through your training sessions. It points you to the most appropriate practice based on whatever is coming up for you on a given day or in a particular practice session. When you follow the Map to Self-Compassion, every training session is custom-tailored for you, based on your own particular strengths and obstacles.

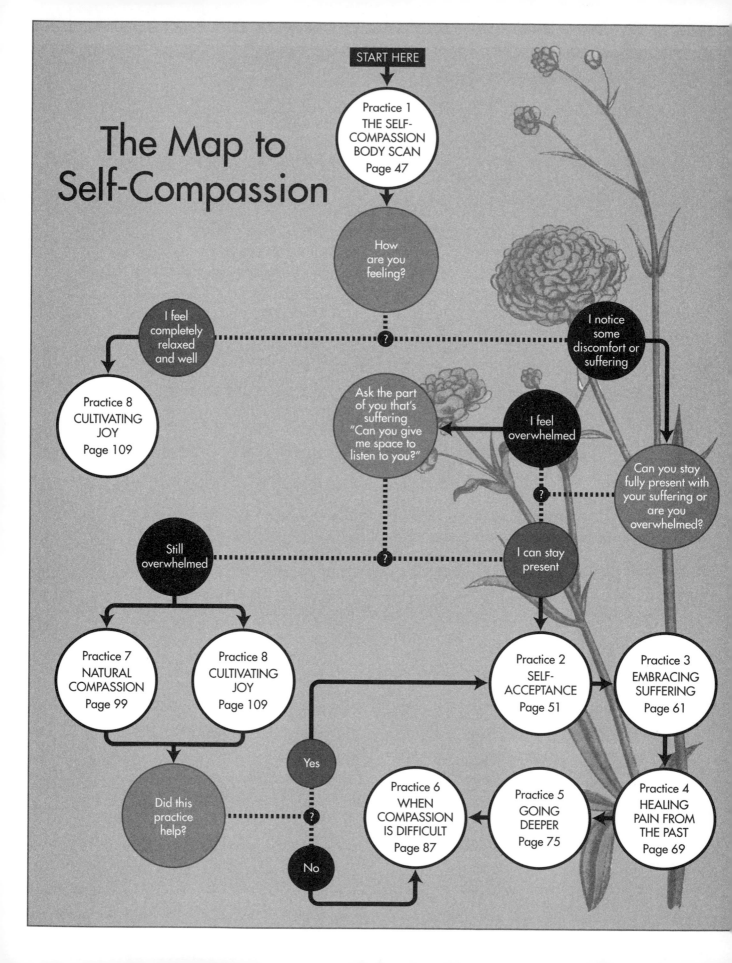

How to Use the Map

You begin each training session at the top of the Map with Practice 1: The Self-Compassion Body Scan (explained in detail in Chapter 5). Then you follow the Map by answering specific questions about your experience. For example, if you begin a training session and you are feeling totally relaxed and well, you are guided to skip to Practice 8: Cultivating Joy. If you notice some distress or discomfort in your body (but not so much that it's overwhelming), then you are guided to Practice 2: Self-Acceptance.

If you want, you can go through each practice in the workbook and try it out before attempting to follow the Map. This might help you develop a sense of familiarity with the entire process and how it fits together.

Begin each self-compassion training session with Practice 1: The Self-Compassion Body Scan. Then follow the Map to Self-Compassion to find the most appropriate practice for you.

Once you begin your 14-day program, use the Practice Journal at the end of this chapter to keep track of the duration of your practice sessions (I suggest 30 minutes per day), which practices you used, and your personal notes about what happened. When you've completed your 14-day program, you can decide how much time each day you want to devote to your ongoing practice of self-compassion.

When and Where: Tips for Setting Up Your Practice Sessions

You can set up your practice sessions any way you'd like. However, here are some suggestions that many people find helpful:

— Try to schedule your training sessions at the same time each day. This will help you create a rhythm and make it easier to be consistent.

— Try *not* to schedule any commitments immediately after your training sessions. Many people find these practices bring up strong emotions, and it's helpful to have some downtime afterward.

— Try to schedule your training sessions so you won't be disturbed. Turn off your phone, and put away anything that could distract you.

— Social support can make these practices much easier. If you let friends or family know you are engaging with this training, they might be able to offer encouragement or other types of help. Consider looking online for a local meditation group. You can refer to Chapters 6, 7, and 8 for more about social support.

— This workbook has some space for you to write responses as you're practicing, but it will fill up after one or two training sessions. You can use separate paper or a dedicated journal for writing your responses to each practice.

If You Feel Overwhelmed

The practices in this workbook are powerful, and they can bring up intense emotions. This is usually a good thing, because it can mean you are experiencing deep transformation. However, it is also possible to become overwhelmed by intense feelings so that you can no longer process them effectively. During your training sessions, it's ideal for your emotions to be strong but not overwhelming. As a general guideline, the level of emotional intensity should ideally be between 4 and 8 out of 10. If it's below 4, then it's probably not deep enough to create real change. If it's over 8, it's likely too intense to process effectively.

If you become overwhelmed at any point during a training session, go directly to Practice 7 or 8 to ground yourself and restore a sense of safety, or just take a break and relax. The following are a list of symptoms that indicate you are overwhelmed and no longer processing emotions effectively. DO NOT CONTINUE a practice if you begin experiencing any of the following:

— Highly elevated heart rate
— Excessive sweating
— Rapid breathing
— Chest pain
— Uncontrollable trembling or shaking
— Sensation of choking
— Feeling of unreality or detachment from your surroundings
— Nausea
— Feeling confused
— Feeling overwhelmed by your emotions in general

These symptoms can mean that your body and brain have moved into a fight-flight-freeze response. When that happens, emotional processing is no longer effective. Before continuing, you'll need to take whatever space you need to feel safe and calm.

Finding the Right Balance

Self-compassion practice shouldn't feel like a chore. It shouldn't be something you do because you're supposed to, or something you have to endure in order to feel better later. If you approach self-compassion training in this way, it won't be as helpful as it could be.

Instead, try to relate to these training sessions as a treat you are giving to yourself. There is a saying in Buddhist circles about meditation: good in the beginning, good in the middle, and good at the end. We know that we are practicing correctly because our training feels like a relief right away—good in the beginning. As we continue practicing, even when intense suffering comes up, we embrace it in a way that feels healing—good in the middle. Then, when we realize how these practices have changed us, we feel grateful—good in the end.

If this isn't how you feel when you're practicing, I suggest that you stop your practice and rest for a few days. Then, try to revisit the Map to Self-Compassion with fresh eyes and see if you might have been staying with one practice, when another one would have been more appropriate.

There are two sides to self-compassion training:

1. Cultivating joy and compassion (Practices 7 and 8)
2. Embracing suffering (Practices 2 through 6)

It's important to find the right balance between these two categories of practice. If you're spending too much time with the first and neglecting the second, you'll notice that the changes you experience seem a little superficial. You might have learned how to find peace in yourself when you're alone, but the deep source of your suffering remains unchanged. It continues to come up, and you feel like you have to practice constantly to keep it at bay. If this is the case, you need to focus more on embracing your suffering with understanding and compassion to transform it at its roots.

On the other hand, if you focus exclusively on the second category and neglect the first, your practice will feel exhausting. It will feel like you have spent hours getting in touch with your suffering, but no real transformation has occurred. Your practice will feel uninspired, routine, and like a chore. This is because we need to cultivate a reservoir of compassion and joy within us. These energies act like a source of fuel that enables us to be fully present with our suffering. The purpose of Practices 7 and 8 is to help you fill your reservoir of joy.

Self-Compassion Assessment Quizzes

You can take these quizzes before and after your 14-day training program to measure your progress. The first quiz measures the strength of suffering in you. Self-compassion has the power to embrace and transform suffering, so you might find that your score goes down after your training program. The second quiz measures the strength of compassion in you, so the program is designed to help that score increase. If you find this program was helpful, you can continue indefinitely.

Quiz 1: The Strength of Your Suffering (Circle the numbers that apply to you.)					
	Never	**Rarely**	**Sometimes**	**Often**	**Always**
I feel depressed.	1	2	3	4	5
I feel anxious.	1	2	3	4	5
I feel angry.	1	2	3	4	5
Pain or trauma from my past has a negative impact on day-to-day life.	1	2	3	4	5
I don't like myself.	1	2	3	4	5
Total score:	Add the circled numbers from above and enter the total to the right:				

Quiz 2: The Strength of Your Compassion (Circle the numbers that apply to you.)					
	Never	**Rarely**	**Sometimes**	**Often**	**Always**
I motivate myself with kindness rather than criticism.	1	2	3	4	5
When I'm suffering, I can actively send myself compassion.	1	2	3	4	5
I believe that a compassionate person would love and accept me if they really knew me.	1	2	3	4	5
I know how to use compassion to heal pain from my past.	1	2	3	4	5
I am kind and compassionate to parts of myself that seem irrational.	1	2	3	4	5
Total score:	Add the circled numbers from above and enter the total to the right:				

Practice Journal

Begin each of your practice sessions with Practice 1: Self-Compassion Body Scan. Then follow the Map to Self-Compassion to find the most appropriate practices for you. Use this journal to keep track of the date, length of your practice sessions, which practice(s) you used, and notes about what came up for you. If possible, try to set aside 30 minutes a day for 14 days in a row for your practice sessions.

Day No.	Date	Length of session (in minutes)	Which practice(s) used (1–8)	Notes
1				
2				
3				

Day No.	Date	Length of session (in minutes)	Which practice(s) used (1–8)	Notes
4				
5				
6				
7				
8				

Day No.	Date	Length of session (in minutes)	Which practice(s) used (1–8)	Notes
9				
10				
11				
12				
13				

Day No.	Date	Length of session (in minutes)	Which practice(s) used (1–8)	Notes
14				

The Practices

THIS CHAPTER PROVIDES DETAILED INSTRUCTIONS FOR HOW TO DO THE EIGHT practices in the Map to Self-Compassion. The practice instructions correspond to various tracks on "Guided Meditations for Self-Compassion," which you can find online at http://www.selfcompassionworkbook.com/.

THE SELF-COMPASSION SKILLS WORKBOOK

Practice 1

The Self-Compassion Body Scan

Each session of self-compassion training should begin with this practice. It will help you to assess your emotional state and determine the most appropriate next step in your training session.

Practice Instructions

 The following practice instructions correspond to track 1 on "Guided Meditations for Self-Compassion," at http://www.selfcompassionworkbook.com/.

Arrange yourself in a comfortable posture. You can have your eyes open or closed, whichever feels more comfortable.

— *Mindful Breathing (3–10 breaths).* Bring your attention to the physical sensation of your breath coming in and going out. Follow the entire breath, from the beginning to the end. Don't try to change how you are breathing at all. Just pay attention to your breath, and let it be however it wants to be. Allow yourself to stop everything else in your life. Let go of the past and future, and allow your breath to bring your mind into the present moment. Practice this until you can remain focused on the sensation of your breath for at least 3 entire breaths, from the beginning of your in breath until the end of your out breath.

— *Mindfulness of the Body (at least 3 breaths, and up to 5 minutes).* Allow your awareness to expand from the sensation of your breath to your entire body. With each breath, you focus your attention on all of the sensations in your body as they arise and pass away. Notice any tension or relaxation; any heaviness or lightness; any sensation at all. Scan your entire body. Write down all the sensations you notice in your body. For example, "tension in my shoulders," "heaviness in my heart," or "agitation in my whole body."

_____

_____

_____

_____

_____

_____

_____

_____

_____

_____

_____

Body-Scan Practice – Questions

Now that you have assessed the sensations that are present in your body, use the following questions to determine which practice to use next.

Do you notice any tension, agitation, heaviness, or any other form of discomfort in your body?

— **No.** If you don't find any discomfort in your body—which means you feel completely relaxed and open—then go to Practice 8: Cultivating Joy. This will help you strengthen the wellness you already feel.

— **Yes.** Do you find the discomfort overwhelming? Do you feel exhausted? Are you able to stay present with it?

- **Overwhelming.** If it is overwhelming, try asking the part of yourself that feels distressed, "Can you step back a little so I can listen to you and try to help?" If that works, go to Practice 2: Self-Acceptance. If it still feels overwhelming, go to either Practice 7: Natural Compassion or Practice 8: Cultivating Joy, which will help you regulate the intensity of your feelings.

- **Exhausted.** This could indicate that your reservoir of joy and compassion is running low. If so, go to either Practice 7: Natural Compassion or Practice 8: Cultivating Joy.

- **Can stay present.** If you can stay present with it, go to Practice 2: Self-Acceptance.

Body-Scan Practice – Examples

Here are a few examples of what this practice can look like. The main point here is to notice whether any distress is present in your body, and then to use the questions above to choose your next practice.

— Oren closes his eyes and focuses on his breath. He pays careful attention to the physical sensations as his breath comes in and goes out. After 3 breaths, he imagines his awareness expanding to fill his entire body. As he does so, he notices tension in his face and a heavy feeling in his heart. He takes a few breaths and asks himself, "Is this overwhelming, or can I stay present?" Finding that he can stay present with this level of discomfort in his body, he goes to Practice 2: Self-Acceptance.

— When Janelle tries to focus on her body, she doesn't notice any sensation at all. She asks herself, "Am I feeling relaxed and well?" and it's clear that she is not. She just can't feel anything. Then she asks herself, "Am I feeling numb?" and immediately realizes that she is. Since she doesn't feel overwhelmed, she also goes to Practice 2.

— Joanne has been practicing with the Map to Self-Compassion for almost a year. She spends 30–45 minutes a day, 5 or 6 days per week, with her practice sessions. When she sits down and brings her awareness to her body, she feels deeply relaxed and happy. She spends about 10 minutes paying close attention to her body, waiting to see if there is any distress that might want to arise, and enjoying the pleasant sensations that are present in her. Then, she moves to Practice 8: Cultivating Joy, to make her happiness deeper and more stable.

— As Bruce tries to focus on his breath, he feels distracted and uneasy. After a few breaths, he tries to pay attention to his whole body, but he's overwhelmed with panic. When he tries to name what he is feeling, he just pops out of the exercise. Bruce knows this often happens to him when he tries to be present in his body, so he isn't worried. He just skips to Practice 7: Natural Compassion, to calm his agitation.

Now, after you've completed the Practice Instructions for this chapter, use the Body-Scan Practice Questions to determine which practice to do next.

Practice 2

Self-Acceptance

The purpose of this practice is to be fully present with whatever sensations arise in your body, or whatever thoughts arise in your mind. You learn to embrace these sensations and thoughts with compassion and mindfulness, rather than struggling against them or being carried away by them. Whether your thoughts and bodily sensations are pleasant, unpleasant, or neutral, you welcome them with open acceptance.

Once you have developed the ability to greet each thought and bodily sensation with compassion and acceptance, you'll find that you no longer get caught up in negative thoughts or feelings. They can come and go without disturbing your peace of mind.

There are two basic types of self-acceptance:

— *Mindfulness of the Body*: We focus on all the sensations in the body with open acceptance. Whether pleasant, unpleasant, or neutral, we allow all sensations to arise and pass away in their own time.
Mindfulness of Thoughts: We notice our thoughts as they come and go. Rather than believing them or arguing against them, we recognize that they are thoughts and let them arise and pass away in their own time.

Mindfulness of the Body

In this practice, we relate to our emotions as sensations in the body. There are both bodily sensations and thoughts that relate to nearly every emotion. For example, when you feel afraid, a big part of that experience involves some type of discomfort in your body (maybe tightness in your throat, heaviness in your chest, or shakiness throughout your body). There might also be fearful thoughts, but for this exercise we focus only on bodily sensations. Experiment with this practice and see if you find it to be helpful.

MINDFULNESS OF THE BODY PRACTICE –
TIP: STAGES OF MINDFULNESS

The image that my teacher, Thich Nhat Hanh, uses to describe mindfulness of the body is of a mother embracing her newborn baby with all her warmth and loving presence. We are learning how to embrace whatever experience arises in us with that kind of love. However, this can be difficult, especially at the beginning of our training.

For many of us, the best we can do is to tolerate the sensations in our bodies. We have spent many years struggling against them or trying to avoid them through various forms of distraction and addiction. Now, when we come home to our bodies, just tolerating our feelings is a big step for us.

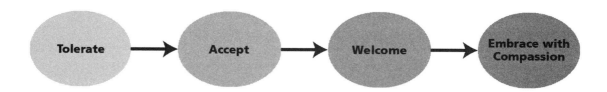

It can be helpful to use the diagram above to think about how mindfulness practice deepens over time. We might begin by merely *tolerating* the sensations in the body. After some time, we develop *acceptance*. We might think, "I don't need to make these feelings go away. It's OK for me to feel them." Later, we can *welcome* our feelings. We might now think, "Hello, anger. I'm here for you and willing to pay attention to you." And eventually, we learn how to *embrace* our feelings with warmth and love. We think, "Dear sadness, I see that you are present, and I am so happy to take care of you."

PRACTICE INSTRUCTIONS

 The following practice instructions correspond to track 2 on "Guided Meditations for Self-Compassion," at http://www.selfcompassionworkbook.com/.

Arrange yourself in a comfortable posture. You can have your eyes open or closed, whichever feels more comfortable.

Bring your attention to all the sensations in your body. Pay special attention to your face, head, chest, and belly.

— Do you notice any tension in your body?
   ☐ Yes.
   ☐ No.
   if yes, Where? _____

— Do you notice any relaxation in your body?
   ☐ Yes.
   ☐ No.
   if yes, Where? _____

— Do you notice any heaviness in your body?
   ☐ Yes.
   ☐ No.
   if yes, Where? _____

— Do you notice any lightness in your body?
   ☐ Yes.
   ☐ No.
   if yes, Where? _____

— Do you notice any heat in your body?
   ☐ Yes.
   ☐ No.
   if yes, Where? _____

— Do you notice any coolness in your body?
   ☐ Yes.
   ☐ No.
   if yes, Where? _____

— Do you notice any agitation in your body?

☐ Yes.

☐ No.

if yes, Where? _____

— Do you notice any other sensations in your body?

☐ Yes.

☐ No.

if yes, Where? _____

Now, see if you can allow all those sensations to be as strong as they want to be. Allow yourself to feel them completely without trying to make them change at all. The goal of this practice is *not* to make unpleasant sensations go away. Instead, you are allowing yourself to feel whatever sensations arise in your body with total openness and acceptance. They might get stronger, change in some way, or remain the same. You are just watching and feeling. You might say to yourself, "It's OK for me to feel what I'm feeling. I can let it get stronger if it wants to, or fade away. I don't need to fight anything." Write down what you notice. For example, "tension in my heart starts to relax," or "heaviness in my belly gets stronger."

_____

_____

_____

_____

_____

As you begin to pay close attention to the sensations in your body, you'll notice many different ways your mind and body might respond.

— If your thoughts are distracting you from staying present with the sensations in your body, don't fight them or try to suppress them. Go to the *Mindfulness of Thoughts* exercise below.

- If the feelings in your body become so intense that you feel overwhelmed, go to Practice 7 or 8.
- If the sensations in your body get stronger, begin to fade, or new sensations arise, continue *Mindfulness of the Body* practice.

Bring your attention to all of the sensations in your body. With each breath, allow yourself to feel whatever arises. If the sensations in your body are pleasant (like relaxation, warmth, or openness), give yourself permission to enjoy them. If they are unpleasant (like tension, agitation, or heaviness), try to embrace them with open acceptance. Feel them and let them be as strong as they want to be. Every feeling that arises in your body is OK. See if you can allow yourself to be open to all of them. You might say to yourself, "Whatever feelings arise in my body are OK, whether they're pleasant, unpleasant, or neutral. I'm not trying to change anything. My only job is to be open and feel whatever comes up in myself." Continue this practice for 5–10 minutes. Whenever you notice a change, write it down.

_____

_____

_____

_____

_____

_____

_____

_____

MINDFULNESS OF THE BODY PRACTICE – QUESTION

After a few minutes of practicing like this, is your distress or discomfort still present or has it gone completely?

- — **Still present.** Go to Practice 3: Embracing Suffering.
- — **Gone.** Go to Practice 7 or 8, to deepen your wellness and joy.

MINDFULNESS OF THE BODY PRACTICE – EXAMPLE

Oren completes the Self-Compassion Body Scan and notices tension in his face and heaviness around his heart. He then shifts to *Mindfulness of the Body* practice and gives himself time and space to feel the tension and heaviness within him. As he brings his attention to his body, the heaviness gets stronger. Oren isn't worried, because he knows that he's not trying to make it go away. He's just letting himself feel it. After about 10 breaths, he starts saying to himself, "It's OK for me to feel this. It can be as strong as it wants to be." Just then, he feels the tension and heaviness begin to release. He tells himself, "It's OK if this fades away, and it's OK if it comes back. I'm open to feeling whatever arises." After 10 minutes of practicing, Oren feels deeply peaceful.

Mindfulness of Thoughts

Most of us believe that everything we think is true, which is kind of crazy. When we look back, it's easy to see how often our thoughts and perceptions haven't been totally accurate. Despite this, however, we still believe the next thought that pops into our heads.

Mindfulness of thoughts helps us to develop a more rational and realistic relationship with our thinking. In reality, our minds create thoughts all day long, as well as much of the time we are sleeping. The mind analyzes and comments on everything that happens to us, and even comments on its own commentary. There is nothing wrong with this. It's what the mind is supposed to do.

The problem comes when we treat a *thought* as though it were a *fact*, especially because the mind doesn't wait until it has all the information it needs before forming a thought. Imagine if your mind didn't create thoughts until you had all the information you needed to accurately understand something. That would be a very different situation, and probably rather difficult to function in daily life.

With mindfulness of thoughts, we learn to recognize that *thoughts are thoughts*—no more and no less. They are useful sources of information, but they should always be taken with a grain of salt.

There are many different ways to train ourselves in mindfulness of thoughts, but for the purpose of this program you will use this practice only when strong thoughts are distracting you from being able to practice mindfulness of the body.

Practice Instructions

 The following practice instructions correspond to track 3 on "Guided Meditations for Self-Compassion," at http://www.selfcompassionworkbook.com/.

Arrange yourself in a comfortable posture. You can have your eyes open or closed, whichever feels more comfortable.

As you are practicing mindfulness of the body, thoughts will arise that make it difficult to stay concentrated on your bodily sensations. When this happens, the first thing to do is to recognize that a thought is present, and name it as a thought. Don't argue with it or try to make it go away. Recognize that it's just a thought, and allow it to stay or go however it wants. Then return to mindfulness of the body practice.

PRACTICING WITH DIFFERENT TYPES OF THOUGHTS

Different kinds of thoughts respond better to different ways of practicing. Here are some examples:

— Aversion to bodily sensations. For example: You are trying to practice being open to tension in your body, and the thought comes up, "I hate this tension."
  - You might say to yourself, "Of course you hate this tension. That's perfectly OK. It's possible to allow the thought 'I hate this tension' to be present, and allow the tension to be present as well." When this type of thought arises, it can be helpful to empathize with this part of yourself. For example, you could say "It's OK for me to hate this tension. That's perfectly natural." Then, see if you can allow the thought to be present *and* allow the sensations in the body to be present *at the same time*. They are both happening within you, so you give them both permission to be there.
— Aversion to mindfulness practice. For example: "This practice isn't helping me."
  - Some of us have been avoiding our feelings for a long time. When we finally come home to ourselves, we might find a great deal of pain waiting for us. It is only natural that your mind will say, "Let's stop doing this and do something more pleasant." In this situation, you also empathize with that part of yourself by saying something like, "Of course you don't like this. You'd rather feel something more pleasant, and that is natural." Then you gently tell yourself that this practice will actually lead to much greater well-being, if you can embrace your suffering with love. Here you're saying, "There is a part of me that is suffering, and I want to take care of it."

— Thoughts unrelated to the emotion you're experiencing. For example: "Don't forget to buy dish soap."

  - This could be your mind making sure you don't forget something important, or it could be a random association. It might also be your mind's attempt to avoid feeling your suffering, or it could be part of your normal stream of consciousness. In this situation, just acknowledge the thought, name it as a thought, and return to the sensations in your body. If your mind is worried you'll forget something, you can take a moment to write it down before letting it go. If it is an attempt to avoid your suffering, treat it like the "aversion to bodily sensations" example above—allow the unrelated thought to be present *and* allow the emotion you're experiencing to be present at the same time.

— Stories you are telling yourself. For example: "I know I'm going to get fired," or "I wish she would just love me."

  - Practicing with this type of thought can be tricky. Often the content of these stories is not entirely based in reality. If you recently had an argument with your daughter, for example, you might have thoughts like, "She hates me," or "I'm such a jerk." When a thought like this arises, we still don't argue with it or try to make it go away. However, it can be helpful to say to yourself, "I'm having a thought that might or might not be true. I don't need to decide if it's true right now. I'm just accepting whatever comes up in me." We all have thoughts like this from time to time. Freedom and peace of mind don't come from eradicating them. They come from accepting that our thoughts aren't always accurate, and learning how not to get caught in our thinking.

MINDFULNESS OF THOUGHTS PRACTICE – QUESTION

After embracing your thoughts with mindfulness, are you able to return your attention to the sensations in your body?

— If yes, return to mindfulness of the body.

— If not, continue to Practice 3: Embracing Suffering.

Practice 3

Embracing Suffering

When you experience the feeling of compassion, the Care Circuit in your brain releases oxytocin and natural opiates. It also dramatically reduces every form of mental distress (and many forms of physical distress, as well). This practice uses your brain's Care Circuit to relieve stress, anxiety, depression, and other negative emotions.

The practice of Embracing Suffering is much more effective after you have spent at least a few minutes practicing Self-Acceptance, as described in the previous chapter. You begin by accepting all your bodily sensations and thoughts without trying to change them in any way. This deep acceptance is the best foundation for generating compassion.

Every human being suffers. It is something that we all have in common. We all experience loss, frustration, and anxiety at different times in our lives. We know what it's like to feel lonely, sad, and angry. However, most of us have never learned the art of embracing our suffering with compassion so that it is transformed into peace and understanding. That's the purpose of this practice.

There are two types of embracing suffering:

1. *Receiving compassion from someone else*: We picture someone—a person we've known, a religious figure, a beloved animal such as a pet, or even an image from nature—and visualize them loving and accepting us. They can be expressing their compassion in whatever way feels most impactful to us, such as holding us, saying loving words, or just looking at us. The important part of this practice is that they are sending us compassion *while we are suffering*.

2. *Sending compassion to yourself*: You recognize the suffering present in your body and mind. Then you express compassion toward yourself. You might say loving words to yourself, place your hand on your heart, or wrap your arms around yourself in a hug. You might imagine an energy of compassion that is directed toward the places in your body where you feel suffering. Again, you do whatever feels the most impactful to convey love and caring to yourself.

Receiving Compassion From Someone Else

The following example illustrates the first type of embracing suffering with compassion.

PRACTICE EXAMPLE

Tina places both hands on her heart and becomes aware of the grief and loneliness within her. She feels those feelings as a weight in her chest and nausea in her stomach. After a few breaths of feeling those feelings without trying to change them at all, Tina visualizes her grandmother. She lets the image of her grandmother become very clear in her mind, and immediately notices some relief in her body. She visualizes her grandmother saying to her, "May you be peaceful. May you be loved," over and over again. With each repetition, she feels the suffering in her body melt away until she feels peaceful and well.

PRACTICE INSTRUCTIONS

The following practice instructions correspond to track 4 on "Guided Meditations for Self-Compassion," at http://www.selfcompassionworkbook.com/.

Arrange yourself in a comfortable posture. You can have your eyes open or closed, whichever feels more comfortable.

In the last exercise, Self-Acceptance, you became aware of the suffering that is present in your body. Whatever form this distress is taking—whether it's anger, fear, sadness, frustration, loneliness, tension, heaviness in the body, or anything else—you recognize that it is there. In this practice, as in the previous one, you are not trying to make your suffering go away. You remain grounded in a deep acceptance of yourself and everything you are experiencing. Describe how you are experiencing your suffering right now.

_____

_____

_____

_____

_____

_____

_____

_____

_____

Now see if you can picture someone—a person you've known, a religious figure, an animal, an archetype (imaginary person), or even an image from nature—and visualize them loving and accepting you right in this moment. They can see how you are suffering and they are filled with compassion for you. Write down the person you choose:

_____

(Note: If you can't imagine anyone loving and accepting you, go to Practice 4: Healing Pain From the Past.)

Now continue to concentrate on that person. Let the image be very clear. Some people like to use a photo or other physical image if they have a difficult time visualizing. Recognize how they love and accept you right in this moment that you are suffering. Notice the sensations in your body.

Do you notice relaxation? ☐ Yes.
                              ☐ No.
Do you notice tension?   ☐ Yes.
                              ☐ No.
Do you notice lightness? ☐ Yes.
                              ☐ No.
Do you notice any other sensation?   ☐ Yes.
                                     ☐ No.
                                     What?

_____

(Note: If you notice tension or any other form of distress in your body, go to Practice 6: When Compassion Is Difficult.)

Continue to concentrate on that person and allow the positive feelings in your body to become as strong as they want to be. The person can express acceptance and love in whatever way feels most impactful to you. Pay attention to the positive sensations in your body, and try saying to yourself, "It's alright to feel this. I can let this feeling be as strong as it wants to be."

(Continue for 1–3 minutes.)

Now picture that person saying the following phrases to you (feel free to use other phrases if these aren't helpful).

— May you be happy.
— May you be healthy.
— May you be safe.
— May you be loved.

Picture the person saying these phrases a few times and allow the positive feelings in your body to be as strong as they want to be. Write down whether the positive sensations in your body have grown stronger or have changed in any way.

— Grown stronger?   ☐ Yes.
                    ☐ No.
— Changed?   ☐ Yes.
                    ☐ No.
                    If changed, can you describe how so?

_____

_____

_____

_____

Continue this practice for another 5–10 minutes.

Sending Compassion to Yourself

 The following practice instructions correspond to track 5 on "Guided Meditations for Self-Compassion," at http://www.selfcompassionworkbook.com/.

PRACTICE INSTRUCTIONS

Arrange yourself in a comfortable posture. You can have your eyes open or closed, whichever feels more comfortable.

In the last exercise, Self-Acceptance, you became aware of the suffering that is present in your body. Whatever form this distress is taking—whether it's anger, fear, sadness, frustration, loneliness, tension or heaviness in the body, or anything else—you recognize that it is there. In this practice, as in the previous one, you are not trying to make your suffering go away. You remain grounded in a deep acceptance of yourself and everything you are experiencing. Describe how you are experiencing your suffering right now.

_____

_____

_____

_____

_____

Now place your hands on your heart, on the sides of your face, or anywhere that feels comforting. See if you can direct the energy of love and compassion toward yourself in this moment. Focus especially on the places in your body where you feel your suffering. You might try saying to yourself, "I see that you are suffering, and I am here for you." As you practice in this way, notice the sensations that arise in your body. Write down what you notice:

Do you notice relaxation? ☐ Yes.

☐ No.

Do you notice tension? ☐ Yes.
                        ☐ No.
Do you notice lightness? ☐ Yes.
                          ☐ No.
Do you notice any other sensation? ☐ Yes.
                                    ☐ No.
                                    What sensation?

_____

(Note: If this practice isn't feeling helpful to you right now, go to Practice 4: Healing Pain From the Past.)

Continue to concentrate and allow the positive feelings in your body to become as strong as they want to be.

(Continue for 1–3 minutes.)

Now try saying the following phrases to yourself. Feel free to use other phrases if these aren't helpful.

— May you be happy.
— May you be healthy.
— May you be safe.
— May you be loved.

Write down whether the positive sensations in your body have grown stronger or changed in any way:

— Grown stronger? ☐ Yes.
                   ☐ No.
— Changed?   ☐ Yes.
                   ☐ No.
                   If changed, can you describe how so?

_____

Continue this practice for 5–10 minutes.

PRACTICE QUESTION

Did you have a strong positive experience with either of these practices?

— If yes, continue with these practices for the rest of the time you've allotted for this training session.

— If not, try Practice 4: Healing Pain From the Past.

Practice 4

Healing Pain From the Past

If we imagine a 100-year-old tree, we can see that the 50-year-old tree is contained within it. We could count the rings and point to the exact place where the 50-year-old tree is present in the 100-year-old tree. We can see that the 20-year-old tree and the 10-year-old tree are all concretely present in the 100-year-old tree.

It is the same with us. Every experience we have is recorded in the shapes of connections in the neural networks in our brains. If a past experience is still impacting us in any way, it's because the connections that were made during that experience are still concretely present in our brains. Someday brain imaging technology may become so accurate that we will be able to identify the exact place where our brain stores the experience of our 5-year-old self being humiliated by an older sibling, or our 10-year-old self being bitten by a neighborhood dog.

This is why healing the past is possible. We cannot change what happened in the past, but we can change how it impacts us. The metaphor of the rings in a tree illustrates how the past can be accessed in the present because its marks remain within us. We can access how those experiences are stored in our brains and change them.

In fact, neuroscientists have demonstrated that the key to transforming pain from the past is to get in touch with that pain while experiencing compassion *at the same time*. This triggers a process in your brain called *memory reconsolidation* that literally rewrites your emotional response to a past experience. The memory isn't erased; it is simply changed so that it doesn't cause distress anymore.

For this type of deep transformation to occur, all we need to do is to get in touch with pain from our past *as well as* our compassion for ourselves—both at the same time.

- Just bringing up pain with no compassion is the same as continuously ruminating, which only causes the pain to get worse.
- Just bringing up compassion with no pain is the same as doing Practice 7 or 8, which builds joy and regulates emotions but is not transformative.
- Bringing up pain and compassion *together* can lead to deep transformation.

The purpose of this practice is to heal and transform the pain from your past.

Healing the Past Practice – Example

Darrel was emotionally abused by his parents when he was a child. He now suffers from insecurity and self-criticism. As he begins this practice, he allows himself to get in touch with his insecurity as a shrinking feeling and the sense of wanting to cry. He feels this in his body for a few breaths—just allowing himself to feel it. Then he reflects on the first time he felt this way. He remembers a moment when he was very young (he thinks around 5) when his father was yelling at him and his mother wouldn't look at him. As he recollects that image, the feelings in his body become stronger.

Now he imagines standing next to this sad and lonely 5-year-old boy, and feels a well of compassion arise in him. He tells the little boy that he is perfect, and that his parents are only like that because they haven't learned how to be kind to anyone. It is not the little boy's fault. He expresses to the boy that he loves him very much and wants to help him. The boy seems relieved, and Darrel spends nearly an hour feeling this connection with himself as a little boy. When he ends his practice, he notices a profound sense of peace in himself.

Practice Instructions

The following practice instructions correspond to track 6 on "Guided Meditations for Self-Compassion," at http://www.selfcompassionworkbook.com/.

Arrange yourself in a comfortable posture. You can have your eyes open or closed, whichever feels more comfortable.

Become aware of the suffering that is present in you in this moment. Whatever form this distress is taking—whether it's anger, fear, sadness, frustration, loneliness, tension or heaviness in the body, or anything else—you recognize that it is there. In this practice, you are not trying to make your suffering go away. You are grounded in deep acceptance toward yourself and everything you are experiencing. Describe how you are experiencing your suffering right now.

_____

_____

_____

_____

_____

_____

_____

_____

_____

_____

As you are feeling this suffering in your body, ask yourself, "When was the first time I can remember feeling this exact feeling?" It doesn't need to be the first time ever, just the first time you can remember. Write down a brief note about the specific memory or general time period that arises:

_____

_____

_____

_____

(Note: If you start to feel overwhelmed, go to Practice 8: Cultivating Joy.)

Picture yourself at the age you were in that memory. Do not visualize yourself during a traumatic event. Instead, just picture yourself at that age. You are still your present self, and you are looking at your past self. No one else is around in this scene. Look at your past self and pay attention to the expression on your past self's face. Notice the feelings that come up for you and what you feel like saying to your past self. Write down these feelings and what you feel like saying:

_____

_____

_____

_____

_____

_____

_____

_____

_____

(Note: If your feelings or words could be considered caring or compassionate, continue with this exercise. However, if you feel angry, blaming, or indifferent toward your past self, go to Practice 6: When Compassion Is Difficult.)

Now express your compassion to your past self. You might say what you've been feeling, or interact in some other way. Consider telling your past self that he or she is lovable and does not deserve to be treated badly. Alternatively, you can imagine someone else who symbolizes great compassion expressing their love for your past self. Notice how your past self responds. Does he or she accept the affection? Seem defensive or argue? Write down a brief description of the interaction:

_____

_____

_____

_____

_____

Continue to dialogue with your past self until you are sure that he or she can receive your compassion. Then go on expressing your compassion in whatever way feels most powerful to you. Pay attention to the sensations in your body as you express your love.

Continue this practice for 5–20 minutes.

Still picturing your past self, try saying the following phrases. Feel free to change them to something else if these aren't helpful.

— May you be happy.
— May you be healthy.
— May you be safe.
— May you be loved.
— You are completely lovable.
— You do not deserve to be treated badly.

If these phrases make your experience of compassion stronger, then continue this practice for 5–10 minutes. If not, express your love to your past self in your own way.

Healing the Past Practice – Question

Did you have a strong positive experience with either of these practices?

— If yes, continue with these practices for the rest of the time you've allotted for this training session.
— If not, try Practice 5: Going Deeper.

Practice 5

Going Deeper

My meditation teacher Thich Nhat Hanh describes mindfulness practice using the image of a mother holding her newborn baby. We can learn how to bring this type of warm and loving presence to our own experience.

However, although this kind of loving presence is often healing and transformative, sometimes we need to go deeper.

When a baby is crying, if her mother picks her up and holds her with complete presence and compassion, the baby might begin to feel better right away. Yet sometimes loving attention alone isn't enough. If the baby is still crying, the parent will try to figure out what is wrong. Is the baby hungry, wet, tired, or is it something else? This is a process of active inquiry into the cause of the baby's suffering. Then, once the parent understands the cause, he or she will naturally take action to address it. It is the same with mindfulness practice.

If we embrace our suffering with compassion, sometimes that's all we need in order to feel better. Other times, however, there is a deeper cause that needs to be addressed. In this case, we use a practice of active inquiry, trying to look deeply enough to understand the root causes of our suffering. After we gain this new understanding, we can then see the most beneficial action we can take to address the problem.

The three primary ways of going deeper are as follows:

1. *Listening to Suffering in the Body*: We get in touch with our suffering as sensation in the body. After embracing it with acceptance and compassion, if we don't feel anything shift we begin to ask those bodily sensations what they need us to hear. Go to this practice if you've been relating to your suffering mainly as bodily sensation.

2. *Listening to a Past Self*: We are in touch with a past self that is suf-

fering. After attempting to direct love and compassion to this past self, if we don't feel anything shift we can ask "What do you need me to hear?" Go to this practice if you were able to get in touch with a past self who is suffering but didn't respond completely to Practice 4: Healing Pain From the Past.

3. *Listening to Parts of Yourself*: As we are practicing, we might notice persistent thoughts, distractions, or even resistance to compassion. Some part of ourselves is not cooperating with the way we've been trying to practice. If this has been your experience, go to this practice.

Listening to Suffering in the Body Practice

 The following practice instructions correspond to track 7 on "Guided Meditations for Self-Compassion," at http://www.selfcompassionworkbook.com/.

PRACTICE INSTRUCTIONS

Arrange yourself in a comfortable posture. You can have your eyes open or closed, whichever feels more comfortable.

Become aware of the suffering that is present in your body in this moment. Whatever form this distress is taking—whether it's tension, heaviness, agitation, numbness, or anything else—you recognize that it is there. Notice if it is located in a particular part of your body, or if it's everywhere. In this practice, you are not trying to make your suffering go away. You are grounded in deep acceptance of yourself and everything you are experiencing. Describe how you are experiencing your suffering right now.

_____

_____

_____

_____

_____

_____

_____

_____

Now you will experiment with addressing questions to this sensation in your body. This practice might or might not feel relevant to you at this time, and that's fine. We're just experimenting. You will ask a few different questions to the sensations in your body, and just listen for a response. We aren't answering these questions intellectually. We're seeing if you notice a spontaneous response when you address them to the suffering in your body. Now become aware again of the sensations in your body associated with your suffering, slowly ask the following questions, and write down whatever information that comes into your awareness:

— How are you trying to help?
— What is your job?
— What do you need me to hear?
— What do you need?

Write down what your suffering tells you:

_____

_____

_____

_____

_____

_____

_____

_____

_____

LISTENING TO SUFFERING IN THE BODY PRACTICE – QUESTION

During this type of practice, your suffering will either express a positive intention (it's trying to meet a need, it wants your help, it's trying to protect you, etc.) or it will express hostility.

— If you hear hostility, go to Practice 6: When Compassion Is Difficult.
— If you hear a need or positive intention, engage in compassionate dialogue with this part of yourself.

LISTENING TO SUFFERING IN THE BODY PRACTICE – EXAMPLE

Barbara sits down on her meditation cushion and closes her eyes. She focuses her attention on the sensations in her body, and becomes aware of something she describes as feeling like a heavy stone in her gut. She feels close to crying. Barbara has explored Practices 2–4 in this workbook, and the stone feels unchanged. So she asks the stone in her gut, "What is your job?" She senses an inner voice saying, "I don't have a job." She tries the question, "What do you need?" and hears the response, "I don't know. I'm just so deeply alone."

Barbara intuitively places both of her hands on her belly and says, "I understand. I'm here with you now, and I will listen to whatever you want to tell me." She feels the stone dissolve as a huge wave of sadness and loneliness floods through her body. Barbara isn't overwhelmed, however, and she allows herself to feel these feelings. For the next 20 minutes she slowly repeats, "I hear that you feel alone. I'm here with you now. I'll listen to anything else you want to tell me." Eventually, she feels the sadness fade and leave behind a sweet calmness and comfort that she's never felt before.

Listening to a Past Self

 The following practice instructions correspond to track 8 on "Guided Meditations for Self-Compassion," at http://www.selfcompassionworkbook.com/.

PRACTICE INSTRUCTIONS

Arrange yourself in a comfortable posture. You can have your eyes open or closed, whichever feels more comfortable.

Become aware of the suffering that is present in your body in this moment. Spend at least 10 breaths feeling this sensation in your body without trying to change it. Now, reflect on the first time you can remember feeling this way. Get a clear mental image of yourself at that age. Pay close attention to the expression on your past self's face. Notice the feelings that come up in you as you let yourself become fully present with your past self. Try saying, "I am here to listen to you." If your past self responds in any way, write down the response:

_____

_____

_____

_____

_____

_____

_____

_____

_____

_____

Now you will experiment with asking your past self a few questions. This practice might or might not feel relevant to you at this time, and that's fine—we're just experimenting. You will ask a few different questions of your past self and just listen for a response. We aren't answering these questions intellectually. We're just seeing if you notice a spontaneous response when you address them to your past self. Now, slowly, ask these questions of your past self and write down whatever information you hear:

— How do you feel?
— Why do you feel like that?
— Is there anything I can do to help you?
— What are you doing to keep yourself safe?
— Is there anything you want to tell me about what I should do to stay safe?

Write down what your past self tells you:

_____

_____

_____

_____

_____

_____

_____

_____

_____

_____

LISTENING TO A PAST SELF PRACTICE – QUESTION

Does your past self respond positively to your willingness to listen?

— If yes, continue to dialogue with your past self for as long as it feels helpful. Experiment with going back to Practice 4: Healing Pain From the Past if your past self seems more open to receiving compassion from you now.

— If your past self says anything self-critical or reacts negatively to your kindness, go to Practice 6: When Compassion Is Difficult.

LISTENING TO A PAST SELF PRACTICE – EXAMPLE

When Medea tried expressing love and compassion to her 6-year-old self, the little girl seemed to distrust her affection. Medea stayed with the visualization and asked her little girl, "Are you afraid?" The girl said, "Yes." Then Medea asked, "What are you doing to keep yourself safe?" and the girl responded that if she lets her guard down, someone will attack her. Medea empathized and told the girl how sad it made her to hear that people have been cruel to her. Then Medea explained that she (her adult self) has the power to prevent anyone from hurting the little girl ever again. Through this dialogue, Medea's 6-year-old self started to become willing to trust. When the girl's guard finally began to come down, Medea went back to expressing love and compassion for her. After 25 minutes of that practice, Medea felt exhausted and took a long nap. When she awoke, she felt a profound shift in how she felt about herself and a deeper sense of confidence than ever before.

Listening to Parts of Yourself

 The following practice instructions correspond to track 9 on "Guided Meditations for Self-Compassion," at http://www.selfcompassionworkbook.com/.

PRACTICE INSTRUCTIONS

Arrange yourself in a comfortable posture. You can have your eyes open or closed, whichever feels more comfortable.

As you begin to bring your attention to the sensations in your body, notice whatever thoughts, distractions or resistance might arise. Pay attention to whatever form this distraction or resistance is taking. Try saying to yourself, "There is a part of me that doesn't want to practice self-compassion in this way." If this feels true to say, then allow yourself to get in touch with that part of you. You might feel it is located in a certain part of your body, or that it has some kind of form or color. When you are in touch with this part—when you feel that it is present—ask this part of yourself, "What is your job? How are you trying to help?" Write down anything you notice in response:

_____

_____

_____

_____

_____

_____

_____

_____

_____

LISTENING TO PARTS OF YOURSELF PRACTICE – QUESTION

Can you see the *positive* intention in that part of yourself (for example, it wants to protect you or prevent you from feeling too much pain)?

— If you can, then continue your dialogue with it. Try to empathize with this part of yourself, *and* to help it to understand your perspective. Continue with this practice until the end of this training session.

— If you don't hear any response, or if this part is hostile or critical, go to Practice 6: When Compassion Is Difficult.

LISTENING TO PARTS OF YOURSELF PRACTICE – EXAMPLE

When Corey was trying to send compassion to the suffering in him, he kept feeling ashamed of himself. He knew that he desperately needed self-compassion, because he was convinced that his tendency to criticize his girlfriends came from deep insecurity. He wanted to be kinder in relationships, so he was very motivated to practice. However, when he tried to send compassion to himself (or visualize someone else doing so) his feelings of insecurity would get even more intense.

Then he arrived at the practice of listening to parts. He asked his insecurity, "What is your job? How are you trying to help?" and it became immediately clear that this part of him was trying to protect him from being ridiculed. The first response Corey heard was, "If anyone saw you doing this, they would laugh at you."

Corey saw this as protective, rather than a hostile response, so he tried to have a dialogue with it. He thought that his most recent ex-girlfriend would be so happy to see him meditating and getting in touch with his feelings, so he asked that part, "Do you think everyone would laugh, or just some people." The part responded, "Anyone who matters." He paused and thought about who would laugh, and his father was at the top of the list. He asked the part, "Are you scared of what Dad would think if he saw us?" and he felt a surge of fear throughout his body and heard a "Yes."

Corey visited his father only once or twice a year, and they almost never spoke. After reflecting on what he had just learned from this inner dialogue, Corey decided that he didn't want to base his life on his father's opin-

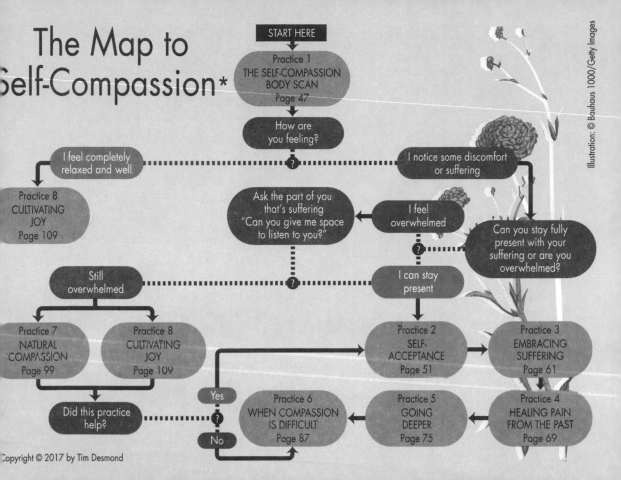

The Map to Self-Compassion*

START HERE

Practice 1
THE SELF-COMPASSION
BODY SCAN
Page 47

How are you feeling?

?

I feel completely relaxed and well

I notice some discomfort or suffering

Practice 8
CULTIVATING
JOY
Page 109

Ask the part of you that's suffering "Can you give me space to listen to you?"

I feel overwhelmed

Can you stay fully present with your suffering or are you overwhelmed?

?

Still overwhelmed

I can stay present

Practice 7
NATURAL
COMPASSION
Page 99

Practice 8
CULTIVATING
JOY
Page 109

Practice 2
SELF-
ACCEPTANCE
Page 51

Practice 3
EMBRACING
SUFFERING
Page 61

Did this practice help?

Yes

?

No

Practice 6
WHEN COMPASSION
IS DIFFICULT
Page 87

Practice 5
GOING
DEEPER
Page 75

Practice 4
HEALING PAIN
FROM THE PAST
Page 69

Copyright © 2017 by Tim Desmond

Illustration: © Bauhaus 1000/Getty Images

The Map to Self-Compassion

The Map to Self-Compassion is designed to point you to the most appropriate training practices based on whatever is coming up for you on a given day or in a particular practice session.

How to Navigate the Map

Begin each training session at the top of the Map with Practice 1: The Self-Compassion Body Scan (explained in detail in Chapter 5 of the book).

From there, follow the Map to your next practice by answering questions about your experience. For example, if you begin a training session and you are feeling totally relaxed and well, you are guided to skip to Practice 8: Cultivating Joy. If you notice some distress or discomfort in your body (but not so much that it's overwhelming), you are guided to Practice 2: Self-Acceptance.

Research shows that anyone can develop self-compassion. All that is required is a willingness to practice. Devote 30 minutes a day for 14 days to this form of training. You will see significant (and often life-changing) results.

W·W·NORTON

NEW YORK · LONDON

ions anymore. He spoke to the part again saying, "It's true that Dad would laugh, and maybe even get angry, but he's an old fool anyway. If we keep trying to please him, we'll never find love." Then a torrent of emotion flowed through Corey's body—terror, exhilaration and relief. He practiced self-acceptance, allowing himself to feel all this emotion without any resistance. After 35 minutes of sitting with all these feelings, he finally felt peaceful and unafraid. He put his hands on his heart and sent himself the energy of compassion without any worry about what anyone might think. Once he was feeling more peaceful, he didn't even feel the need to call his dad a fool. He could see that his dad suffers a lot and feels really lonely. Finding compassion for himself naturally led to compassion for his father.

Practice 6

When Compassion Is Difficult

Self-compassion can be difficult, but in my experience, it is always possible. Whatever obstacle that might prevent us from experiencing self-compassion can be overcome, and the secret for doing so is deceptively simple. We learn how to embrace the *obstacle itself* with compassion and understanding.

In the practice of compassion, there are no enemies. We are peacemakers, who are committed to finding ways to understand and embrace whatever thoughts, feelings and sensations arise within us. This might not be easy, but it's much easier than constantly being at war with ourselves. We begin this practice by consciously calling for a ceasefire.

To be clear, we *do not* passively surrender to the darkest parts of ourselves. We don't give in to self-hate or despair. We don't allow these parts to control us. Yet neither do we seek to annihilate these parts of ourselves. We have learned that hating our hatred just creates more hatred. In the end, we see that these parts of ourselves are like crying children. They aren't being rational, and shouldn't be put in charge of anything. What they need is love, understanding, and a commitment to repair whatever relational bond has been broken. This is a practice of active nonviolence and of conflict resolution—in our relationship with ourselves.

The more you understand the obstacle that is blocking your self-compassion, the easier it will be to transform it. There are two basic types of obstacles: *overwhelm* and *competing commitments*.

Overwhelm as an Obstacle to Self-Compassion

Overwhelm is the simpler of these two obstacles to overcome, because it mainly requires getting more rest and recuperation. It takes a lot of energy to be present with suffering. If we aren't replenishing the reservoir of joy and compassion within us, we will run out of energy and become exhausted. If you are experiencing uncontrollable grief, feelings of despair, or an inability to stay present with your suffering, you might be overwhelmed.

The primary step for practicing with overwhelm is to remove yourself from stress and get some rest, both physically and psychologically. Physical rest may simply mean catching up on sleep, but it might also include recreational activities or spending time in nature. Do whatever has worked in the past to help you regain your energy and feel more centered and grounded. It is important during this time to completely stop any attempt to embrace your suffering. Instead, set aside an uninterrupted period of time to focus on Practice 7: Natural Compassion and on Practice 8: Cultivating Joy.

If you are well rested and have tried these two practices but are still having a hard time getting in touch with feelings of peace and joy, then it is likely that you are dealing with a *competing commitment* (explained below).

Competing Commitments as an Obstacle to Self-Compassion

Competing commitments are more complicated obstacles to deal with than feelings of overwhelm, but overcoming them is potentially more transformative. Competing commitments refer to the ways we act that seem irrational and self-destructive. We might criticize ourselves, blame ourselves, or refuse to accept the things that could truly help us. However, when we look more deeply, we can see that these "negative" or "destructive" parts of ourselves are actually suffering and desperately in need of compassion.

We all have many different parts of ourselves. For example, it's possible to feel attracted to something and afraid of it at the same time, or to want something and wish that you didn't. This ambivalence doesn't mean that your brain is malfunctioning or that you have a psychological problem. On the contrary, it is actually an important part of how a normal brain works.

Scientists now understand that our brains perform many different functions all at the same time. In fact, there might be more than a billion distinct processes happening in your brain right now. Your brain is regulating your heartbeat, maintaining your sense of balance, running your immune system, scanning for potential threats to your survival, translating light on your retinas into letters, letters into words and ideas, and then testing to see how those ideas relate to your life experience. The human brain is truly amazing.

Ideally, all these different processes work together in harmony. When they do, you feel like you are a unified person who thinks consistent thoughts and feels in a consistent way. However, conflicts in our thoughts and feelings often arise and create all sorts of problems.

Here's an example to clarify what I mean:

When Mitchell came to see me for therapy he had been struggling with depression for quite some time. He had read several self-help books and seen a few other therapists with no noticeable improvement. Nonetheless, he was still highly motivated to start feeling better, and willing to try any suggestion.

As Mitchell and I were talking about his history, he explained that he had grown up in a family that would ignore him when he was doing well, but would become very affectionate and caring when he got depressed. As soon as I heard that, the term *competing commitment* flashed across my mind.

The Harvard psychologist Robert Kegan coined the term *competing commitment* to describe how different parts of the same person can want different things. In Mitchell's case, *one part* of him truly wanted to feel better, but I was beginning to suspect that *another part* of him (a part he had no idea existed) might actually be afraid of letting his depression go.

It was clear that Mitchell was not conscious of any desire to remain depressed. He was adamant that he would do anything to feel better. However, when he explained that there was a time in his past when the only way to get caring attention was to be depressed, it made me wonder if there might be some part of him that still believed being depressed was a good way to get love. The only way to know for sure was to explore the issue experientially, so I used a practice like the one you'll try later in this chapter.

I asked Mitchell to get in touch with his depression, and feel it in his body. He described it as a sinking feeling in his whole body that made him want to lie down. Once he was feeling it, I asked him to try a sentence completion exercise. I gave him the first part of a sentence, and asked him to finish it with whatever popped into his mind, even if it didn't make sense. I said, "Try finishing the sentence, 'I can't let go of my depression, because if I do . . .' and say whatever pops into your head. We'll do this a few times."

The very first thing that Mitchell said confirmed my suspicions. He said, "I can't let go of my depression, because if I do I will disappear." He was completely surprised by this sentence, so I asked him to repeat it a few times out loud and see if it continued to feel true. He said, "I can't believe it, but it really feels true. There's a part of me that thinks no one will notice me if I stop being depressed. Am I crazy?"

I said, "Of course you're not crazy. You grew up in a family in which that was the reality. Whenever you stopped being depressed, your family would ignore you. Even though there's a big part of you that doesn't want to be depressed, it sounds like there is another part of you that believes people won't notice you *unless* you're depressed. That's very normal, and we just need to help that other part of you to understand that you are not living with your family anymore. Those old strategies used to work, but they don't work now."

I asked him to repeat the sentence a few more times ("I can't let go of my depression, because if I do I will disappear.") and let me know how old he felt while he was saying it. He said that he felt about 7 years old, so I asked him to visualize himself as a 7-year-old boy. When he had a clear image of that little boy, we told him that we were *proud of him* for figuring out how to get his needs met in his family. It took a lot of intelligence to discover that being depressed was the best way to get care and love. The boy was happy that we recognized his strengths. Then we told him that not everyone was like his family. This was shocking to the 7-year-old, who had assumed no one in the world would notice him unless he was depressed. We told him that many other people are actually *more loving* when you *aren't depressed*. We continued the dialogue until the 7-year-old boy seemed to understand and believe us.

This was a profoundly transformative experience for Mitchell. Before our work together, he felt powerless over his depression. He believed he was desperately trying to change, but that he wasn't strong enough. Then, he discovered an entirely new part of himself. It was a part that had an *important purpose* for holding onto his depression.

Richard Schwartz, the psychologist and originator of Internal Family Systems, would call this part a *manager*. Its job was to protect Mitchell by keeping him depressed so that people would continue to care about him. The more he tried to get rid of his depression, the more forcefully this part would protect it. He was caught in an internal struggle because he didn't recognize this part's existence.

When we discovered this part of Mitchell, we didn't punish or blame it. Instead we empathized with it. We did our best to express appreciation for how this part believed it was doing an important job, and then we shared a vital piece of information that it had obviously not known—that many people can care about you when you aren't depressed.

Here are the main steps from this process. (I will provide guided instruction to help you try this for yourself in a moment.)

1. Get in touch with your suffering or whatever obstacle to self-compassion you've found. Feel it in your body.

2. Use some inquiry practice (like sentence completion) to help that part of you articulate why it believes the obstacle is important to maintain.

3. Once you can understand *why* that part of you wants to keep your obstacle to self-compassion, try to identify how old that part of you is. You might repeat the sentence that describes the purpose of your obstacle, and notice how old you feel when you say it.

4. Visualize yourself at that age and acknowledge how this obstacle was actually a realistic strategy at that time.

5. Then explain to your younger self why this strategy is no longer needed.

When I describe competing commitments to groups of people, I find there tend to be two types of responses. Some people say, "Oh, of course. That makes perfect sense." Others say, "That sounds crazy. It certainly isn't true for me." I do not expect you to believe there is a competing commitment in you merely because you've encountered some obstacles to self-compassion. Rather, I invite you to experiment with the practices below and see for yourself.

The two most important concepts in working with competing commitments are as follows:

1. There is a part of you that believes it is *more important* to keep your obstacle to self-compassion than to let it go. That part of you sees an *important purpose* in maintaining the obstacle.

2. We don't seek to eradicate the part of you that is holding onto your obstacles. Instead, we want to understand why that part believes its job is so important. We want to treat that part with compassion and to dialogue with it in a loving way.

Here are some common types of obstacles to self-compassion. You might have experienced one or more of these in the practices you've attempted so far.

— When you visualize yourself in the past (often as a child), you blame your past self for your suffering.

- When you visualize yourself in the past, your past self refuses to believe he or she wasn't to blame for your suffering.
- There is a voice in you that is hostile or critical toward you, and you haven't been able to reconcile with it.
- You've experienced strong feelings of distress in your body when attempting self-compassion.

Here are some common reasons people hold onto self-criticism. Read each one and notice if it resonates with you.

- *Maintaining connection.* If I realize that I never deserved to be abused, then my parents become horrible people. If I deserved the abuse, I can continue feeling connected with them.
- *Maintaining the illusion of control.* If I am to blame for the abuse, then I can control it by becoming better. If I'm not to blame, then it is entirely outside my control—and that is scary.
- *Maintaining fairness.* If I'm not to blame for the abuse, then I live in a world in which good people can be hurt without having done anything wrong. That would feel too unfair.
- *Protecting a relationship.* If I believe that I am lovable, someone important in my life will reject me. This person believes that I deserve disrespect and could not tolerate it if I were to disagree.
- *Avoiding responsibility for life.* If I know there is nothing wrong with me, I become responsible for my life. Believing I'm broken allows me to escape responsibility.

PRACTICE INSTRUCTIONS

The following practice instructions correspond to track 10 on "Guided Meditations for Self-Compassion," at http://www.selfcompassionworkbook.com/.

(Note: If you become emotionally overwhelmed at any point during this practice, stop and rest. You can use Practice 7: Natural Compassion and Practice 8: Cultivating Joy to regulate intense feelings. It can also be helpful to do this practice under the supervision of a trained mental health professional.)

Arrange yourself in a comfortable posture. You can have your eyes open or closed, whichever feels more comfortable.

You have come to this practice because you've experienced some kind of obstacle to self-compassion. Write down the form this obstacle has taken, such as intense self-critical thoughts or blaming yourself for abuse:

_____

_____

_____

_____

_____

_____

_____

Now allow yourself to get in touch with that obstacle. If it came up during a visualization practice, try that same visualization again. Do whatever you need to do to bring it up. We don't want it to be overwhelming, but just strong enough that you can feel it. When it is present, write down what sensations you notice in your body:

_____

_____

_____

_____

As you are in touch with your obstacle and these feelings in your body, try saying these sentences to yourself and see if any of them feel true, "There is a part of me that doesn't want to stop feeling like this or doing this to myself. There is a part of me that needs to hold onto this. There is a part of me that thinks I deserve this." Write down which sentence felt true (if any) and anything else that came up for you:

_____

_____

_____

_____

Continue feeling those feelings in your body, and feeling in touch with this part of yourself. Try saying to yourself, "I'm ready to listen to you. You can tell me about your job, what you are trying to do and why it is so important. I'm not going to attack you." Write down whatever comes up:

_____

_____

_____

_____

_____

_____

_____

_____

Now try this sentence completion. Just write down whatever pops into your head, and do it at least 5 times. Finish the sentence:

"I refuse to have compassion for myself because if I do . . ."

1. _____

_____

_____

"I refuse to have compassion for myself because if I do . . ."

2. _____

_____

_____

"I refuse to have compassion for myself because if I do . . ."

3. _____

_____

_____

"I refuse to have compassion for myself because if I do . . ."

4. _____

_____

_____

"I refuse to have compassion for myself because if I do . . ."

5. _____

_____

_____

Choose the one or two sentences from the sentence completion exercise that feel the most emotionally powerful to you. Repeat them a few times (aloud or silently) and notice *how old* you feel when you say them. Write down how old you feel (if there is a specific scene, include that):

_____

Visualize yourself at that age. Once you have a clear image of your past self, spend a few minutes trying to understand and empathize with this part of yourself. Can you see how this part believed it was helping you or meeting an important need? You can dialogue with your past self and ask any questions you need to ask in order to understand the important purpose for the belief, feeling, or behavior. Once you see this, acknowledge how it was actually a realistic strategy at that time, and express appreciation for how your past self was doing an important job. Write down what you notice:

_____

_____

_____

_____

_____

_____

_____

Now tell this part of yourself whatever important information it doesn't know. What does this part of you need to know in order to recognize that it doesn't need to continue blocking self-compassion in your life? (Often this has to do with your present life being so much different from your life as a child.) Continue dialoguing with this part until there is a mutual understanding. This part will be willing to stop doing its job once you communicate that you understand *why* it thought its job was so important, and once you are able to convince it that its job is no longer necessary. Spend as much time as you need to communicate this. Write down what happens:

_____

_____

_____

_____

_____

_____

_____

_____

_____

_____

COMPETING COMMITMENTS PRACTICE – QUESTION

Did you discover a part of yourself that had a purpose for blocking self-compassion?

- If yes, were you able to empathize with this part of yourself?
  - If yes, continue directing compassion to this part of yourself for at least 10 minutes.
  - If not, rest or spend some time with Practice 8: Cultivating Joy. Then attempt this practice again, or do so under the supervision of a trained mental health professional.
- If not, try this practice under the supervision of a trained mental health professional.

Practice 7

Natural Compassion

The practice of natural compassion can be used in several ways:

— It can be used as a way to exercise your brain's Care Circuit and improve your ability to generate compassion. It's like doing pushups for your Care Circuit.

— It can be used as a preliminary practice—getting you ready to direct compassion toward yourself. When self-compassion is hard, this practice is easier.

— It can also be used to ground you and regulate powerful emotions if you are feeling overwhelmed in any way—whether the emotions arise during self-compassion training or in your daily life.

There are three basic types of natural compassion practice:

1. *Sending Practice*: We choose some recipient—a person, animal, or anything at all—and send love and compassion to it.

2. *Receiving Practice*: We picture someone—a person we've known, a religious figure, or even an image from nature—and visualize them loving and accepting us.

3. *Sending & Receiving Practice*: We choose someone and alternate between sending and receiving as we breathe. Breathing in, I receive compassion. Breathing out, I send compassion.

Sending Practice

 The following practice instructions correspond to track 11 on "Guided Meditations for Self-Compassion," at http://www.selfcompassionworkbook.com/.

PRACTICE INSTRUCTIONS

Arrange yourself in a comfortable posture. You can have your eyes open or closed, whichever feels more comfortable. You might place your hands on your heart, wrap your arms around yourself in a hug, or place your hands on the sides of your face.

Explore different objects—it can be a person, animal, or anything—until you find one that brings up natural and uncomplicated feelings of warmth and love. Write down the object you chose. You might also draw a picture of it, or find a photo or printed image you can hold:

_____

_____

_____

_____

_____

Now continue to concentrate on your object. Let the image be very clear. Notice the sensations in your body. Do you notice relaxation, tension, or lightness? Write down the body sensations you notice:

_____

_____

_____

_____

_____

(Note: If you notice tension or any other form of distress in your body, skip this exercise and go to Receiving Practice.)

Continue to concentrate on your object and allow the positive feelings in your body to become as strong as they want to be.

(Continue for at least 10 breaths.)

Now try saying the following phrases to the object you are picturing. Feel free to change these phrases, or not to use them if they aren't helpful.

— May you be happy.
— May you be healthy.
— May you be safe.
— May you be loved.

Repeat these phrases a few times and allow the positive feelings in your body to be as strong as they want to be. Write down the body sensations you notice now:

_____

_____

_____

_____

_____

Continue repeating this practice for at least 5 minutes.

Some people love using phrases with Sending Practice. Others prefer various kinds of visualizations. If you like using phrases, you can use the ones suggested above or you can create your own by experimenting to discover what feels the most powerful to you. Here are some more suggestions:

- May you be peaceful.
- May you have ease.
- May you be joyful.
- May you know that your needs matter.
- May you know that you are beautiful.

SENDING PRACTICE – EXAMPLE

Jeff closes his eyes, puts both hands over his heart, and pictures his dog. He lets the image get really clear and notices the relaxation, warmth and opening in his chest. He stays with this image for a few breaths and then begins to silently repeat these phrases: "May you be happy. May you be loved." He repeats these phrases over and over as the positive sensations in his body grow and he feels on the verge of tears. He stays with this image and his phrases for 20 minutes, really allowing himself to enjoy this state of compassion, love and peace. Jeff uses this practice whenever he's starting to feel depressed or frustrated. He also likes to practice for 10 minutes or so each morning.

SENDING PRACTICE – QUESTION

Did you have a strong positive experience with this practice?

- If yes, continue to practice it for the rest of the time you've allotted for this training session. In your next session, you can choose to begin with Practice 1 or return directly to this practice.
- If not, try Receiving Practice.

Receiving Practice

 The following practice instructions correspond to track 12 on "Guided Meditations for Self-Compassion," at http://www.selfcompassionworkbook.com/.

PRACTICE INSTRUCTIONS

Arrange yourself in a comfortable posture. You can have your eyes open or closed, whichever feels more comfortable. You might place your hands on your heart, wrap your arms around yourself in a hug, or place your hands on the sides of your face.

See if you can picture someone—it could be someone you've known, a religious figure, an image from nature, an animal, or even a white light—who could love and accept you completely. Write down the person you choose:

_____

Now continue to concentrate on that person. Let the image be very clear. Notice the sensations in your body. Do you notice relaxation, tension, lightness, or any other sensation? Write down the body sensations you notice:

_____

_____

_____

_____

_____

_____

_____

_____

Natural Compassion

(Note: If you notice tension or any other form of distress in your body, skip this exercise and go to Practice 6: When Compassion Is Difficult.)

Continue to concentrate on that person and allow the positive feelings in your body to become as strong as they want to be.

(Continue for at least 10 breaths.)

Now picture that person saying the following phrases to you. (Feel free to change these phrases, or not use them if they aren't helpful.)

— May you be happy.
— May you be healthy.
— May you be safe.
— May you be loved.

Picture the person saying these phrases a few times and allow the positive feelings in your body to be as strong as they want to be. Write down the body sensations you notice now:

_____

_____

_____

_____

_____

_____

_____

_____

_____

Continue this practice for at least 5 minutes.

In this practice, it doesn't matter if the person you choose is living or dead, real or imaginary. All that matters is that the visualization is effective at activating the Care Circuit in your brain and generating the feeling of love and compassion.

RECEIVING PRACTICE – EXAMPLE

Carla closes her eyes and pictures her aunt Peggy gazing at her with an expression of complete love and understanding. She sees her aunt saying to her: "May you know that you are loved. May you be peaceful and free." She feels warmth and lightness in her entire body, and she really concentrates on allowing those sensations to grow. She practices like this for 5 minutes, by which time she's feeling deeply peaceful. She uses this practice at least 4–5 times a day, whenever she has a spare moment.

RECEIVING PRACTICE – QUESTION

Did you have a strong positive experience with this practice?

— If yes, continue to practice it for the rest of the time you've allotted for this training session. In your next session, you can choose to begin with Practice 1 or come directly back here.
— If not, go to Practice 6: When Compassion Is Difficult.

Sending & Receiving Practice

 The following practice instructions correspond to track 13 on "Guided Meditations for Self-Compassion," at http://www.selfcompassionworkbook.com/.

PRACTICE INSTRUCTIONS

Arrange yourself in a comfortable posture. You can have your eyes open or closed, whichever feels more comfortable. You might place your hands on your heart, wrap your arms around yourself in a hug, or place your hands on the sides of your face.

Picture someone—a person or an animal—with whom you feel safe and comfortable. Let the image of that person become clear. Write down the person you choose:

_____

With each breath, you will alternate sending and receiving compassion. With each in breath, imagine receiving compassion—either from this other person or from another source. With each out breath, imagine sending compassion to this other person. Recognize that it's possible for both of you to receive compassion and there is no competition. Write down the body sensations you notice:

_____

_____

_____

_____

_____

_____

_____

_____

_____

Continue this practice for at least 5 minutes.

SENDING & RECEIVING PRACTICE – EXAMPLE

Martin pictures his 4-year-old niece. As he breathes in, he feels how much she loves him. As he breathes out, he feels how much he loves her. When he begins this practice, it feels awkward. Martin is not accustomed to feeling very much intimacy. He considers stopping, but decides to persist for at least a few minutes. After several breaths, he notices his body is relaxing and a feeling of warmth is growing in his chest. After 5 minutes, Martin is crying in a way that feels deeply healing. He keeps practicing like this for 40 minutes, feeling more and more grateful for the presence of his niece in his life. The next day, when he has more free time, he practices like this for nearly 2 hours. When he's finished, he feels ready to return to the top of the Map to Self-Compassion and focus on healing himself.

Practice 8

Cultivating Joy

Where does happiness come from? Is it possible to intentionally develop joy? Do well-being and happiness come from being lucky, achieving great things in life, having some in-born trait, or can they be cultivated through practice?

Researchers who study well-being—positive psychologists—have concluded overwhelmingly that happiness comes from a well-defined set of skills and attitudes. As we develop compassion, gratitude, optimism, and mindfulness, we learn that happiness is available in each moment of life. In fact, the present moment is the only place that happiness can be found. If we want to be happy in the future, the best thing we can do is to find happiness in the present.

Researchers have found that contentment and happiness do not come from getting the things we want in life—such as financial wealth, a new car, or career success. In fact, even major external events affect our well-being for only a relatively short period of time. For example, people who win the lottery are back at their previous level of happiness just 6 months after they won, on average. (Better material conditions can have a more lasting effect on happiness, however, for people struggling under poverty or other great hardships.)

It seems clear, therefore, that many of us waste our time looking for happiness in the wrong places. We believe that happiness will be possible only if we can solve this problem or achieve that goal. We think it's something that we can win in the future, but that it could never be possible right now. This perspective prevents us from being happy, and it is the cause of much needless suffering in the world.

Instead of trying to find happiness by improving the external conditions in our lives, we can recognize that happiness comes from developing specific skills—and we can focus our attention on developing them. When we have strengthened our capacity to notice what is beautiful in the present moment, our happiness will no longer be so dependent on the changing conditions in our lives.

The Joy of Mindfulness

One important function of mindfulness is learning to embrace and transform our suffering—which has been the focus of much of this workbook. However, mindfulness can also be a source of joy.

Mindfulness helps us wake up to all of the conditions for happiness that are already available to us in this moment. Many people drink their tea or coffee, but never taste it. Their minds are far away, occupied by worries or regrets. When we learn how to slow down and taste our tea, we find that it is wonderful. Sitting by a tree, walking with a friend, and taking a hot shower on a cold morning are all potential sources of joy, if we know how to pay attention to them.

The Joy of Optimism

Many pessimists believe they are just being rational and realistic, but actually the opposite is true. A pessimistic perspective on life is an entirely irrational position, and I'll explain why.

If you truly want to be rational and realistic, you have to admit that you have no idea what will happen in the future. In fact, we don't know what will happen just 2 minutes from now.

There is a story about a farmer that makes this point very clear. Once there was a farmer whose horse ran away, and all his neighbors came over and said, "What bad luck." The farmer replied, "Maybe." A few days later, the horse came back and brought five wild horses with it. The neighbors came over again and said, "What good luck." The farmer said, "Maybe." Then the farmer's son tried to ride one of the wild horses, but he was thrown and broke his arm. The neighbors said, "What bad luck." And again, the farmer said, "Maybe." Finally the army came through the village conscripting all the able-bodied young men to fight in a war, but they left the farmer's son at home because of his arm. The neighbors came over to say, "What good luck." The farmer said, "Maybe."

Even when something has already happened, we can't know how it will affect us in the future, so the only rational perspective is to admit that we don't know. However, since there is no way to know whether some event in your life will ultimately be good or bad for you, you might decide that it's practical to believe it will be good.

If you lose your job, you might decide to believe that it's a good thing—not because you think you can predict the future, but because that optimistic belief will help you have more energy and enthusiasm in your job search. On the other hand, a pessimistic perspective that expects a negative outcome is not only irrational—since you can't know one way or the other—but it is generally not practical either because it will often hurt your ability to act.

The Practice of Cultivating Joy

There are several ways that you can use this practice:

— If you are feeling peaceful and relaxed after Practice 1: The Self-Compassion Body Scan, this practice can help you deepen your experience of well-being.

— If you feel overwhelmed by the intensity of your suffering at any point during your training, this practice can help you regulate your emotions.

— This practice can help you balance embracing suffering with nourishing your happiness. If you focus too much on your suffering, you can become exhausted. It is important to use this practice to replenish the reservoir of energy you need to bring compassion to your suffering.

CULTIVATING JOY PRACTICE – TIP

You might find that this practice is more effective when you are in a beautiful place, close to nature, or practicing with other people. Explore various settings to find which ones best support you in cultivating joy.

 The following practice instructions correspond to track 14 on "Guided Meditations for Self-Compassion," at http://www.selfcompassionworkbook.com/.

PRACTICE INSTRUCTIONS

Arrange yourself in a comfortable posture. You can have your eyes open or closed, whichever feels more comfortable.

Bring your attention to the sensation of your breath as it comes in and goes out of your body. See if you can follow this sensation from the beginning of your in breath until the end of your out breath.

(Practice for 3–5 breaths.)

Allow yourself to enjoy the sensation of your breath, recognizing that it is a pleasant sensation. Give yourself permission to do nothing but enjoy the sensation of your breath, right in this moment. You have nothing else to do, and nowhere else to go—right now. With a spirit of generosity toward yourself, enjoy the sensation of your breath.

(Practice for 5–10 breaths.)

As you breathe, feel the energy of life within you. You are alive in this moment, and this is a precious gift. Give yourself permission to feel truly alive right now. With each breath, feel the energy of life within you. Every minute of life is incredibly precious. Allow yourself to feel the joy of being alive as you breathe.

(Practice for 5–10 breaths.)

Now imagine that you were in a hospice with just 5 minutes to live—take a moment for that to feel real. Then, someone comes into your room and says they could give you another 24 hours to be alive. It would be such a miracle! In reality, you *do* have 24 hours to be alive, and it *is* a precious miracle. As you breathe, let yourself appreciate each moment of being alive.

(Practice for 5–10 breaths.)

Now become aware of all the parts of your body that are healthy and functioning. We all have parts that hurt or don't function the way we'd like, but there is more to life than just that. There are also many parts of your body that are healthy, and it would be deeply unfortunate to ignore the conditions for happiness that are available to you right now. Can your eyes see the blue sky? Can your ears hear the song of birds and the laughter of children? Can your tongue taste warm tea? Can your body feel the embrace of your loved ones? In every moment there are infinite reasons to suffer and infinite reasons to be happy. Right now, we are dedicating ourselves to paying attention to what is good in life. As you breathe, allow your mind to recollect the miracles of life.

(Practice for 5–10 breaths.)

Now we let go of whatever is preventing us from being fully present in this moment of life. We let go of all of our projects and busyness. Even if these projects are never completed, happiness is still possible. We let go of the past and the future, because we know life is only available in this moment. Feeling fully present, having let go of any burdens, and aware of the miracles of life, you calmly breathe in and breathe out.

(Practice for 5–10 breaths.)

Now bring your attention to the sensations in your body. Notice any tension, relaxation, warmth, openness, or other sensations. Write down what you notice.

_____

_____

_____

_____

_____

_____

_____

_____

_____

_____

CULTIVATING JOY PRACTICE – QUESTION

Through this practice, are you able to generate happiness and well-being in your body? Are the sensations you feel at the end of the practice generally positive?

— If yes, you can use this practice to strengthen your ability to find joy in your life. It can also be used to replenish your energy when you've been focused on embracing suffering.
— If not, go to Practice 6: When Compassion Is Difficult.

Alternative Practices for Cultivating Joy

There are several alternative practices for cultivating joy. You can experiment to see which feel the most helpful for you.

LETTING GO

Arrange yourself in a comfortable posture. You can have your eyes open or closed, whichever feels more comfortable.

Notice any tension or heaviness in your body, and explicitly let it go. With each breath, feel the tension in your body dissolve.

Now ask yourself, "What do I believe that I need in order to be happy? What don't I have that I need?" Listen to yourself for a few breaths and see what answer arises.

Now try saying to yourself, "Even without that, I know that happiness is possible in this very moment. That thing may come into my life if it wants to, but happiness is already available right now."

Let go of the craving in you for reality to be different than it is in any way. Try saying to yourself, "Happiness is possible right here and right now, with the world exactly as it is. Nothing needs to change."

NOTHING TO DO

Arrange yourself in a comfortable posture. You can have your eyes open or closed, whichever feels more comfortable.

As you breathe in and breathe out, allow yourself to stop everything you are doing. Allow your body to stop, and gently invite your mind to stop trying to accomplish anything or fix any problem. Try saying to yourself, "Just for these few minutes, I am choosing to do nothing. I can try to fix, solve, or create things later, but for now, I'm allowed to do nothing." Keep breathing and letting go.

Try saying, "Right now, I am here in this place. There is nowhere else I can be right now. I am here. Right now, I'm not doing anything. Everything in my life can wait a few minutes while I rest and let go. Nowhere to go, and nothing to do."

Remember that happiness is already available to you in this moment. You have everything you need to be happy. You don't have to do anything else in order for happiness to be possible.

INTERBEING

Arrange yourself in a comfortable posture. You can have your eyes open or closed, whichever feels more comfortable.

Focus your attention on the sensation of your breathing. Allow your breath to bring your mind completely into the present moment. Recognizing that all of the conditions needed for you to be happy are already present, you let go of any struggling or striving of any kind. Nothing needs to change. Allow your mind to be calm.

Now become aware of your body. Recognize that every molecule that makes up your body existed before it was part of you. Every water molecule in your blood came into your body in the form of something you ate or drank. Picture yourself sipping a cup of tea. While it is in your cup, it is not your body. Then you drink. Now some of that water becomes part of your body, part of your blood. Even before the water was part of your tea, it existed for a long time in other places. It has been rain, rivers, oceans, and clouds, as it moved through the water cycle. Now it has become part of *you* for a period of time. As you breathe in and out, recognize that every molecule in your body has been soil, stone, or sea. Your body is made entirely of elements that have been other things, and will be again. You realize that you are not separate or cut off from the rest of nature.

Feeling calm, open, and grounded in your conscious breathing, become aware of the presence of your ancestors in you. It's possible to see that your body is a continuation of your mother's and father's bodies. The color of your eyes, the tone of your skin, your height and facial features—it's possible to find your parents' bodies present in all of these parts of you.

You have biological ancestors, and you also have spiritual ancestors. These are the people who have taught you or your family how to live life. All of these ancestors are present in your strengths and abilities. You can see that their strengths and abilities have found a continuation in you. And you can see that their suffering is present in you as well. In many ways, your suffering can be seen as the continuation of the suffering of your ancestors. It's possible to see that every aspect of who you are is the continuation of the strengths as well as the suffering of people who have come before you. Now that you've been exposed to transformative practices, you have the opportunity to choose to cultivate the strengths and happiness in you. You can also choose to embrace and heal the suffering that has been transmitted to you. As you heal this suffering, you heal many generations in the past as well as the future.

PART III

Maintenance

Living Self-Compassionately

Everyday Practice
Peace Is Every Step

IF YOU HAVE BEEN ABLE TO PRACTICE WITH THE MAP TO SELF-COMPASSION for 30 minutes a day for 14 days, that is a wonderful accomplishment. Take a moment to celebrate what you've done. This is an extraordinary investment of time and energy into your own well-being and the well-being of your friends, family, coworkers, and society. It's important to take time to celebrate what is good in life. Otherwise, we miss out on so much beauty and happiness.

Many causes and conditions have contributed to your completing this program. You may have had family members or friends who helped you develop the ability to persist and prioritize when you see something that can help you. You might have experienced some loss or misfortune that prompted you to work on developing self-compassion in your life. The qualities or strengths that helped you arrive where you are today are the product of many positive and negative experiences, as well as your learning from many people. Take a moment to reflect on the various experiences and people that helped you arrive where you are right now, and let yourself feel gratitude for them. You might pause for a few breaths to see how all the causes and conditions in your life have brought you to a place of greater self-compassion.

Moving Forward

Now that you've completed your 14-day program, it's time to consider how you want to incorporate self-compassion practice into the rest of your life. Although scientists have established that just 30 minutes a day for 14 days is sufficient to create measurable changes in your brain and behavior, this is just a taste of what is possible. Those same scientists have shown that the benefits of compassion training continue to expand the longer a person practices. Just as in learning a new language or musical instrument, the more time and energy you invest in developing compassion and self-compassion, the greater the rewards will be.

If you believe—as I do—that self-compassion is a quality with limitless value, then it makes sense to adopt this practice as an important part of your life. Eventually you might find that self-compassion practice stops feeling like just a *part* of your life, and begins to feel more like a guiding principle that informs your entire life. While you might have begun this training with the goal of alleviating depression or changing a specific behavior, the goal of your practice could broaden to responding with compassion to everything in you and around you.

Four Forms of Practice

Once you decide that you want self-compassion practice to be an important part of your life, the next step is to create a way of practicing that fits who you are. I will review four major categories of personal practice, and I recommend trying to incorporate at least one element of each into your life.

DAILY FORMAL PRACTICE

Your daily formal practice can be a powerful anchor in your life. It is the time you set aside each day to deliberately cultivate compassion and self-compassion. It can include sitting meditation, walking meditation, prayer, chanting, studying inspirational or spiritual texts, tai chi, yoga, or listening to the sound of a bell. Part II of this workbook can be an effective guide to your ongoing daily formal practice. However, you can include many other forms as well. It is wonderful if you can continue to devote 20–30 minutes a day to formal practice, but if you can't, 3 minutes is much better than none.

MOMENT-TO-MOMENT PRACTICE

It is also possible to practice self-compassion in every moment of our daily lives—not only while we're meditating, but also while we're walking, driving, doing the dishes, and so on. We can consider this our informal practice, and it can be just as transformative as formal practice.

When my meditation teacher, Thich Nhat Hanh, first became a Buddhist monk in 1942 in Vietnam, he was given a small book of poems. He was instructed to memorize them and recite them throughout each day. There was a poem for waking up, one for putting on his robes, one for washing his face, and so on. This was his introduction to Buddhist monastic training. The poems were reminders to bring mindfulness and compassion to every action and every moment of life. He has adapted these poems for contemporary use in his book *Present Moment, Wonderful Moment*. This is the poem for waking up:

Waking up this morning, I smile.
Twenty-four brand new hours are before me.

I vow to live fully in each moment,
and look at all beings with the eyes of compassion.[xiii]

This is just one example of how we can bring self-compassion into every moment of life. Instead of taking a shower to "get clean," imagine taking a shower in a way that felt like a gift to yourself. Before stepping into the steaming water, you say to yourself, "Now you can enjoy this moment of showering. You have nothing else to do, and nowhere else to go." Even if you are already late for work and can only afford to take a 5-minute shower, those 5 minutes can be a gift that is enjoyed deeply.

When I lead retreats, I often ask people to choose at least one activity that they do each day, and write a little poem to help them do it with self-compassion. It could be getting out of bed, starting your car, or returning home after work. You reflect on how you could perform this action with generosity and compassion for yourself, and you recite your poem to create this awareness during that part of your busy day.

One of the most important practices for me, in my own life, has been paying attention to the sensations in my body throughout the day. I have several specific actions (such as standing up, sitting down, and the end of a conversation) that I use as reminders to pay attention to the current state of emotions in my body. The goal in this practice is to be able to monitor sensations like tension, agitation, and heaviness in my body all day long. The incredible benefit of this practice is the ability to notice suffering when it is still very small and subtle, which makes it much easier to embrace with compassion.

RETREATS

Retreats offer the best possible conditions for developing self-compassion. I think of meditation retreats as analogous to an immersion experience when trying to learn a foreign language. You have a period of time—from one day to several months—in which you are reminded to come back to your self-compassion practice from the time you wake up until you go to sleep.

There are many different types of retreats and retreat centers in the US and around the world. Some retreats, like the 10-day silent retreats you'll find at www.dhamma.org, are very strict and spartan. Some are luxurious, like those offered at Esalen Institute or Miraval Resort. My personal favorite retreats are those offered at Plum Village Monastery and the related practice centers. They are led by monks and nuns who have dedicated their lives to developing mindfulness and compassion, and they include not only sitting meditation, but also singing, outdoor walks, and discussion circles. I believe there is a type of retreat for everyone, and I strongly suggest exploring different retreat centers until you find one in which you feel comfortable.

If you are able to go on a retreat (for a day or longer) each year, that is wonderful. If not, it's possible to have a day of retreat in your own home. Clear your entire schedule for a day, and do nothing other than meditating, reading, journaling, prayer, yoga, and so on. Each day of retreat can provide a tremendous amount of energy that will carry over into your daily practice. Some people even dedicate one entire day a week to rest and retreat.

THE SUPPORT OF A COMMUNITY

Practicing mindfulness and compassion is so much easier with the support of other people. When we practice alone, we must rely on our own willpower to avoid getting carried away by negative habits. In contrast, practicing with a group of like-minded people can create a type of collective momentum that helps us live in harmony with our values.

If you're lucky, you might find a meditation group or a church group that is specifically focused on cultivating self-compassion—and is also a group of people with whom you can feel comfortable. There are meditation communities from many traditions all around the US; the website for finding groups in the Plum Village tradition is www.mindfulnessbell.org/directory/. Most of these groups meet in someone's home and include sitting meditation, walking meditation, and discussion. However, just having one friend or family member who supports your aspiration to develop self-compassion can be extremely helpful as well.

Deepening Your Practice

I hope you find the practices described in this book to be healing and liberating. However, these practices should be viewed only as an introduction to the extensive teachings on mindfulness and self-compassion that are available. I recommend exploring the teachings of Thich Nhat Hanh, Tara Brach, Sharon Salzberg, Kristin Neff, Chris Germer, Paul Gilbert, and Richard Schwartz. Finding teachers that you trust can be incredibly helpful to you on your path.

Thich Nhat Hanh's teaching of "interbeing" is one that can be particularly helpful in cultivating compassion. He coined the term *interbeing* to refer to a special way of perceiving who we are and how we are connected to something much greater than ourselves.

If we believe that we are completely cut off and disconnected from others, it can seem as though there is a conflict between self-compassion and compassion for others. The teaching of interbeing explains how this is a mistaken view.

We can begin to understand interbeing by examining the piece of paper from which you are reading right now. This paper might seem like nothing special, but you are also aware that it used to be part of a tree. Without that tree, the paper couldn't exist. Thich Nhat Hanh would say that the tree is present in the paper if you know how to look deeply.

The tree was made out of sun, soil, and rain. Without any of those things, the tree couldn't exist, so they must be present in the paper as well. At some point the tree was cut down and brought to a factory, so without those workers and all their ancestors, it could never have become paper. If we continue this line of thought, very quickly we can see that everything in the universe has had some role in bringing this paper into existence. Thich Nhat Hanh uses the word *interbeing*, because he says that nothing can *be* by itself. It has to *interbe* with everything else.

Now think about yourself in this way. Every water molecule in your blood came into your body as food or drink. Before that, it was rain, and before that, every bit of water in you has been part of every ocean on the planet. Every calcium molecule in your bones used to be part of the soil.

Every word you use to speak or think was taught to you by someone. Your ideas and perceptions have been shaped by countless people and events. Looking deeply, you can see that the earth, the rain, and innumerable people are present in you. You are deeply connected to something much greater than yourself. Recognizing this, you can see that self-compassion is not selfish at all. It means having compassion for all of these elements that are part of you.

7

Physical Self-Care

SELF-COMPASSION IS NOT ONLY ABOUT CARING FOR OUR THOUGHTS AND emotions. It also means treating our bodies with kindness. Scientists now understand that mental health and physical health are deeply interconnected. If we are under too much psychological stress, our blood pressure goes up, our immune system goes down, our digestion has problems, and we are at higher risk for every kind of malady. The same is true in the reverse direction. If our bodies are too far out of balance (for example, our diet, exercise, or sleep), this can harm our emotional health as well.

This chapter addresses two important elements of caring for our bodies: motivating ourselves with compassion, and finding a balanced lifestyle.

Almost everyone would benefit from using more kindness and less criticism when trying to motivate themselves to make healthy choices. This will be the main focus of the chapter. However, some people will find that changing some aspect of their diet, exercise, or sleep can lead to dramatic improvements in mood as well. I'll share an example of one therapy client whose diet ended up being central to his emotional distress.

I once had a client who was suffering from anxiety. It had gotten bad enough that it was affecting his work, so he came to me for help. After three sessions of exploring various mindfulness, compassion, and relaxation practices, we were getting nowhere and his anxiety was just as strong as ever. Based on the advice of a colleague, I asked about his diet and lifestyle, and I was amazed to learn that he drank eight large cups of coffee each day. He had never thought that caffeine might be affecting his mood. I suggested that he gradually cut down to one or two cups per day, and see if it helped. When I saw him a week later, he explained that his anxiety was completely gone and thanked me profusely (despite experiencing headaches from caffeine withdrawal).

Motivating Ourselves With Compassion

We all want to make healthy choices, but in reality it's not that easy. We're often faced with a conflict between what we know is healthy and what feels good in the moment. Most of us equate making healthy choices with an inner-voice that is critical, harsh, and withholding. The kind and loving voice is usually the one saying, "Go ahead and eat more ice cream. You had a hard day."

There is certainly nothing wrong with treating yourself when you're having a hard time. The issue here is that most of us don't experience the voice that tells us to exercise or eat vegetables as kind and loving, and this can create problems. Instead, the voice advocating healthier choices often sounds like, "I don't care if you're tired. You have to exercise or you'll turn into a (insert demeaning insult here)."

What if we experienced both voices within us as compassionate and caring? There is the voice that says, "You don't always have to do the healthiest possible thing. Sometimes you can choose what feels good in the moment." But imagine if the other voice said, "I don't want you to exercise because you're scared of being unacceptable. Exercise because you know it feels good, it gives you energy, and because that is the kind of person you want to be."

HELPING YOUR HEALTHY VOICE BECOME A KINDER VOICE

Recall a recent time that you felt some inner-conflict about diet, exercise, or sleep. It's likely that one part of you was advocating the choice that would feel good in the short term, and the other was advocating what would be healthier in the long term. Imagine yourself back there for a moment, and get in touch with how these two different voices sounded.

It's likely that the voice that was in favor of short-term comfort sounded kind and soothing. Now pay attention to the other voice—the voice that was encouraging you to make the healthier choice. How was it talking to you? Did it use insults, bargaining, or intimidation? Write down the kinds of things it said.

_____

_____

_____

_____

_____

_____

_____

_____

_____

Now, we're going to try to help that voice express itself in a more compassionate way. See if you can recognize that this part of you is suffering—that it's likely afraid of something. Can you identify the threat that this voice is afraid of? Write it here.

_____

_____

_____

_____

_____

Seeing how this voice in you is suffering, try to recognize that it just wants you to be safe and well. It has a positive intention. Now, try to help this voice in you express its fear and positive intention in a more caring way. Write down the words it might use.

_____

_____

_____

_____

_____

_____

_____

_____

_____

_____

The more you're able to understand this health-advocating voice and encourage it to communicate with kindness and gentleness, the easier it will be for you to follow its suggestions and make those choices.

Finding a Balanced Lifestyle

Some people experience incredibly positive effects from certain lifestyle changes that wouldn't make any difference to other people. For example, some percentage of the population seems to function much better without gluten (from grains such as wheat, rye, and barley). Others seem to require 9 hours of sleep or they're miserable.

Our bodies are different, and what is healthy for you might not be healthy for me. This means we have to experiment to see what kinds of lifestyle changes might be helpful. The problem with most nutrition and lifestyle research is that it's looking for what is good for everyone. That means it can miss the possibility that a minority of us might not respond well to a diet or exercise regime that is great for most people.

For example, I have a friend named Lothar who has always had a tough time sleeping. It seemed that his body really wanted to stay up late and wake up around noon. This made him incredibly groggy in the morning. He had searched high and low for insomnia cures and better alarms, but nothing seemed to help very much. Whatever insomnia cure you might be thinking about right now, it's likely he tried it. Finally, he read that some people are sensitive to *blue light* in the evening—that it affects the hormones that govern their sleeping patterns. He removed all the full-spectrum light bulbs from his home and replaced them with low-blue bulbs, which give off orange or red light. The result was almost immediate. He started getting sleepy around 10 PM and popping out of bed bright and early, which had never happened to him before. I know other people who have tried this same strategy and seen no effect at all. The important point here is that we're all different, and if we're willing to experiment, we might find something transformative.

Now let's look at four major components of a healthy lifestyle and reflect on whether there might be some specific changes that could improve your life.

DIET

There are thousands of conflicting views about what makes a healthy diet. Some are based on excellent research, and some are just fads or worse. I'll focus mainly on areas where most dietary experts agree.

Vegetables are good for you. It's possible for vitamin deficiencies to create mental health problems in otherwise well-adjusted people. Further, scientists are learning that there are many important nutrients that aren't part of multivitamin supplements. So just taking a vitamin pill won't give you all the nutrition that you get from eating whole foods. Therefore, increasing the amount of vegetables in your diet is something that every dietary expert agrees is a good thing. But how many vegetables should you eat? This answer is not totally clear, but it's safe to say there's very little danger of eating too many vegetables. Eat a variety, and as much as you're willing to. Fruits and berries are important sources of balanced nutrition as well.

Too much sugar, caffeine, or alcohol is bad. Some people can function just fine with these substances, but most people experience negative effects from excessive sugar, caffeine, or alcohol. You might consider abstaining from these substances altogether for a couple of weeks and notice whether you feel any better by the end of that time. (If your consumption of these substances is truly excessive, you might need to withdraw from them gradually to avoid headaches and other symptoms of detoxification.) If the idea of total abstinence is scary, that might indicate that you're using a substance for emotional coping. If so, I suggest that you consider phasing it out of your life in favor of using self-compassion.

Do you have a food sensitivity or allergy? Dairy, gluten, eggs, nuts, and soy are just a few examples of foods that are tolerated well by some people but not by others. One of the most common ways to discover if you have a sensitivity to specific foods is to try an elimination diet, which is a process of removing suspected foods from your diet and slowly reintroducing them over a period of several weeks. Unless you are highly knowledgeable about nutrition, it's best to have medical supervision during this period.

EXERCISE

Exercise has been shown to be just as effective as antidepressant medication in treating depression[xiv]. **When experimenting with exercise, however, it's safest to consult your doctor.**

Do you spend too much time sitting down? There is a saying that sitting is the new smoking. Science is learning that spending most of our time sitting at computers has a negative impact on our health and mood. You might experiment with taking breaks every hour or two to move around, or try using a standing desk if you can.

What kind of exercise makes you feel good? Some people love the runner's high they get from aerobic activity. Others prefer playing basketball or some other team sport. Whether you try a spin class or weight training, look for some way of incorporating regular physical exercise in your life in a way that *you actually enjoy*. It could make a huge difference in your day-to-day mood.

SLEEP

The Centers for Disease Control and Prevention (CDC) reports that more than 30% of U.S. adults are suffering from chronic sleep deficiency. This raises our risks for nearly every physical and mental health problem. Personally, when I'm in a bad mood and can't really figure out why I'm so upset, I often take a nap and feel completely better.

Try 8 hours of sleep for 7 days in a row. Some people need more than 8 hours, and some people are fine with a little less. The CDC recommends that no adult sleep less than 7 hours each night. Experiment with giving yourself more sleep than usual for 7 days and see if it makes a difference in how you feel.

Do you have trouble sleeping? After consulting with your doctor, you might try taking a dose of vitamin D in the morning, practicing self-compassion before bed, making your bedroom darker and cooler (65° or cooler, according to many sleep researchers), and getting outdoors to exercise during the day. You might try turning off all devices and screens 1 hour before you go to sleep. Experiment with these ideas and see if they help.

CONNECTION

Feeling connected to others and to something greater than yourself can be a significant source of well-being.

Try volunteering. Many people find that being of service is a great way to feel connected. In fact, there is a large amount of research that shows volunteering can be as effective for reducing depression as therapy or medications. The gratitude you experience and the feeling that you have the ability to make a positive impact in other people's lives can be a source of joy. You might consider the possibility of walking dogs for a local shelter or SPCA, delivering food for Meals on Wheels, spending time at an elder care facility, or volunteering with whatever organization appeals to you.

Try spending some time in nature each day. There is abundant evidence that time in nature supports emotional well-being. There are measurable factors in these studies, such as direct sunlight, better air quality, exercise, and so on. However, the impact of spending time in nature likely goes deeper than that, and relates to the feeling of being part of a greater whole.

8 Compassion and Self-Compassion in Relationships

THE PRACTICE OF SELF-COMPASSION HELPS US TO RECOGNIZE THE BEAUTY OF our own humanity. When we are able to do this, we can then see the same beauty in other people, which makes it easier to feel compassion for them. In this way self-compassion supports our compassion for everyone, strengthens our relationships, and helps us to reconcile and resolve conflicts. This chapter describes how to use self-compassion training to improve all the relationships in your life.

Two Relationship Poisons: Criticism and Demand

Marshall Rosenberg, the creator of Nonviolent Communication, believed that *every criticism is a tragic mis-expression of a need*. In other words, we have an unmet need, and rather than telling people about our need and what they could do to help, we criticize them. This is often because we aren't explicitly thinking about our own need or suffering. Instead, we are evaluating other people and blaming them for their mistakes. He calls this type of thinking "tragic", because the thing that would actually help us feel better—other people understanding us or helping in some way—becomes *less* likely when we criticize them.

Rosenberg also claimed that every demand is a tragic type of request. Demands are tragic because we all wish that people would support us or do things for us simply because they want to, yet this becomes impossible when we make a demand. If I want my wife to listen to me talk about my hard day, what I really want is for her to feel good about listening to me. I want her to enjoy making me happy. If I make a demand, her only choices are to allow herself to be forced into listening to me, or to refuse. My preferred response isn't even an option anymore.

Nearly every conflict or disharmony in a relationship contains criticism or demand. We don't need to feel ashamed about the presence of criticism or demand in us. These are manifestations of our own suffering, and they need our compassion rather than hatred. Fortunately, it's often possible to remove these relational poisons through deep understanding and compassion.

A Practice for Transforming Criticism and Demand

Choose a relationship in which you've been experiencing conflict, and we will explore whether there might be something you could do differently that would help. Admitting that you harbor some criticism or demand toward the other person *does not mean* that you are accepting full responsibility for the conflict. This practice is not about assigning blame. It is about seeing if you can make things better.

(Note: If you are trying to decide whether to end a relationship, this isn't the right practice for you. Rather, it is a practice for when you are certain that you want to make things better.)

If you are sure that you want to stay in this relationship, the first thing to do is to *completely abandon* any attempt to determine who is at fault for the conflict. Instead we are going to focus on whatever piece of the conflict is yours, and attempt to transform it.

ASSESSING CRITICISM AND DEMAND IN YOURSELF

Imagine the other person. Picturing them clearly, do you notice any tension, agitation, or other form of suffering arise in your body? If so, ask yourself if you wish that person were different in some way or would act differently. Do you wish they were kinder, more understanding, or that they would do something you've been asking for? If you recognize *any way* that you wish the other person were different than they are, then it is likely that criticism or demand is present in you.

Reflect on what your criticism or demand might be. A criticism comes in the form of evaluating the other person. There is some way that they are not meeting your approval and you think they should change. What is the criticism you have?

A demand is a strong attachment to the other person behaving in a particular way or doing something differently. What is your demand?

Again, please try not to feel bad if you recognize criticism or demand in yourself. There is nothing wrong with feeling this way, and it doesn't mean you're accepting full responsibility for the conflict. However, if we can identify the roots of your criticism or demand, resolving the conflict becomes much easier.

RECOGNIZING AND HEALING THE ROOTS

Every criticism or demand is the result of an unmet need or emotional pain. Can you identify the suffering in yourself that is fueling your criticism or demand? You might be feeling some grief about a loss from your past. You might be afraid of being rejected. You might deeply want to feel understood and be worried that it won't happen. If so, bring your attention to this pain in yourself and use the practices from Chapter 5 to embrace it with compassion. Allow yourself to feel this pain as sensation in your body *without getting carried away by your stories*. Then direct the energy of love and compassion toward yourself—right at the part of you that is suffering. Continue to practice self-compassion until you feel more peaceful.

Now, while you are filled with self-compassion, imagine the other person again. How does your perspective on the conflict change when you are deeply grounded in compassion for yourself? What happens to your criticisms and demands? In my experience, I'm much better at communicating my needs and listening to others when I'm feeling rooted in self-compassion.

The Beauty in Me and the Beauty in You

I believe that the essence of compassion consists in seeing what is beautiful in oneself and other people. To feel compassion for ourselves, it can be helpful to begin by looking deeply to see the beauty of our own needs, feelings, thoughts, and actions. When we reflect about this, we can see that everything we think, feel, and do is our best attempt in that moment to create happiness or to find relief from suffering.

Here's a story that I believe illustrates how we can find compassion for everyone and even beauty in them. Several years ago, I had a therapy client named James who was having an extramarital affair with a woman named Vanessa. Realizing that the affair was damaging his marriage, he decided that he had to break it off. When he told Vanessa that he wanted to stop seeing her, she threatened that if he did, she would kill herself. He believed that she was just trying to manipulate him, so he decided to break up with her anyway. The day after he ended their relationship, James got a phone call informing him that Vanessa had committed suicide just an hour after he left her apartment.

When he heard this tragic news, he was overcome with both shame and regret. He not only realized that his actions had hurt his wife, but he was also blaming himself for Vanessa's death, and he wanted to talk to me about what had happened.

To be honest, it was hard for me not to blame him as well when I first heard his story. Thankfully, I had been practicing self-compassion for many years, so when I noticed tension in my chest and face, I began to breathe mindfully (as explained in Practice 2: Self-Acceptance). I gave myself complete permission to feel all the sensations in my body, and I sent myself compassion. After a few breaths, I noticed a deep sadness in myself.

I thought about Vanessa's death, and I wished I could have helped her. I saw the depth of despair on James's face, and I deeply wished that I could have prevented this tragedy. There was a part of myself that felt overwhelmed with grief for everything that had already happened, and that part was desperately in need of compassion.

As James was crying, I allowed myself to feel all my sadness, because I knew that if I tried to ignore my own reactions and focus on him, I wouldn't be as present as I knew he needed me to be. I silently told myself, "There are tragedies like this that happen every day in this world, and you can't prevent them all. I know that you would if you could, but it's just not possible." I could see that the part of myself that was suffering so deeply was the part that wanted to help people. There was so much pain and loss in James's story, and that part of me was struggling to accept it.

I empathized with that part of myself, silently saying, "I know that all you want is to help people, and you're afraid you can't do anything to make this situation better. You feel powerless." That was exactly what I needed to hear. I needed to recognize that the aversion in myself came from a desire to help people, and I had to accept that I might be powerless to really change this situation. I was experiencing something that is a universal part of the human condition: I wanted to help but I didn't know how. When I recognized this, I told myself, "You want to help but you don't know how. Everyone feels like this sometimes." This statement released a flood of self-compassion, after which I was able to let go of my judgments about James and see him much more clearly.

I looked at James, and I could see that he was overcome with regret. Then I repeated the statement to myself, "You want to help, but you don't know how," and somehow this acknowledgement opened up a powerful feeling of warmth toward James. I wanted to help him, but I didn't know how. This recognition helped me to be fully present with what was going on with him and with me.

When I looked at him now, I saw a deeply lonely man who had never wanted to hurt anyone. He was lost and didn't know what to do. *We both didn't know what to do*, and this felt like a powerful connection between us. We were both imperfect human beings who wanted to undo what had been done, but we couldn't.

Through the practice of self-compassion, all my resistance to James and what had happened was gone. I could be present and open to all of it, and this allowed me to see James much more deeply. I saw his suffering and his desperate search for happiness, which had been motivating all his decisions. He had looked to Vanessa as a way out of his suffering, but the affair hadn't helped. Then he had left Vanessa to return to his marriage, for the same reason. This whole time he was a sad, lonely, and confused human being, looking for something that could bring him happiness. While you and I might not have made the same mistakes that James did, we've made our own, and for similar reasons.

If we remember that every human being suffers, wants to be happy, but often doesn't know how to find happiness, we can then see something deeply human that we all share. When we can see the beauty in this part of the human condition—that none of us is perfect, but we are all just looking for happiness in our own way—then it becomes possible to find compassion for anyone.

The Greatest Gift You Can Give

In 2005, I was living in Plum Village, Thich Nhat Hanh's monastery in southern France, and I heard him give a talk about a banana tree. He had been asked a question about the meaning of life by one of his students, and responded by telling a story about a deep insight he had experienced while meditating in the jungle in Vietnam many years earlier.

He said that he was sitting by the foot of a young banana tree and contemplating its leaves. It had just three leaves. One was fully grown, broad and flat, and dark green. The second leaf was still partially curled up beneath the first, and the third leaf was very light green and tender, just beginning to unfurl. Looking deeply, he saw that the eldest leaf was fully enjoying her life as a leaf. She was absorbing the sun and rain, radiating beauty and peacefulness. However, she had not abandoned the other leaves to pursue her own happiness. In fact, as she nourished herself, basking in the sunshine, she was also nourishing the younger leaves, the banana tree, and the entire jungle. He went on to explain that human beings are just like this leaf. As we nourish ourselves with peacefulness and compassion, we are also supporting the well-being of every other living thing.

Let's take a moment to reflect on this image. Imagine yourself as this beautiful, fully grown banana leaf. Recognize that, although you are unique, you are also deeply connected to the rest of the tree and to the whole jungle. The more you nourish yourself with the sunshine of serenity and self-love, the more those energies are available to support everyone and everything to which you are connected. As you become more aware of your connection with all that is, you can see that the greatest gift you can give the world is your own peacefulness and happiness.

Reflection Journal

A space to write down your personal reflections, quotes, ideas and anything else you want to remember.

_____

_____

_____

_____

_____

_____

_____

_____

_____

_____

_____

_____

_____

THE SELF-COMPASSION SKILLS WORKBOOK

THE SELF-COMPASSION SKILLS WORKBOOK

Ongoing Practice Journal: Day 15 and Beyond

A space for journal entries and practice notes after Day 14.

Remember: *Begin each of your practice sessions with Practice 1: Self-Compassion Body Scan. Then follow the Map to Self-Compassion to find the most appropriate practices for you. Use this journal to keep track of the date, length of your practice sessions, which practice(s) you used, and notes about what came up for you. If possible, try to set aside 30 minutes a day for your practice sessions.*

Day No. (if you're counting)	Date	Length of session (in minutes)	Which practice(s) used (1–8)	Notes

Day No. (if you're counting)	Date	Length of session (in minutes)	Which practice(s) used (1–8)	Notes

Day No. (if you're counting)	Date	Length of session (in minutes)	Which practice(s) used (1–8)	Notes

Day No. (if you're counting)	Date	Length of session (in minutes)	Which practice(s) used (1–8)	Notes

Day No. (if you're counting)	Date	Length of session (in minutes)	Which practice(s) used (1–8)	Notes

Day No. (if you're counting)	Date	Length of session (in minutes)	Which practice(s) used (1–8)	Notes

Day No. (if you're counting)	Date	Length of session (in minutes)	Which practice(s) used (1–8)	Notes

Day No. (if you're counting)	Date	Length of session (in minutes)	Which practice(s) used (1–8)	Notes

Day No. (if you're counting)	Date	Length of session (in minutes)	Which practice(s) used (1–8)	Notes

Day No. (if you're counting)	Date	Length of session (in minutes)	Which practice(s) used (1–8)	Notes

Notes

i   You can read more about this study at www.mindful.org/how-to-train-the-compassionate-brain/ or read the original research: Weng, H. Y., Fox, A. S., Shackman, A. J., Stodola, D. E., Caldwell, J. Z., Olson, M. C., . . . Davidson, R. J. (2013). Compassion training alters altruism and neural responses to suffering. *Psychological Science, 24*(7), 1171–1180.

ii   Learn more in Panksepp, J., & Biven, L. (2012). *The archaeology of mind: Neuroevolutionary origins of human emotions*. New York, NY: Norton.

iii Learn more from Davidson, R. J. Neuroplasticity: Transforming the mind by changing the brain. In *Mind and Life Conference XII: Neuroplasticity: The Neuronal Substrates of Learning and Transformation, October* (pp. 18–22).

iv   Ibid.

v   Panksepp, J., & Biven, L. (2012). *The archaeology of mind: Neuroevolutionary origins of human emotions*. New York, NY: Norton.

vi   Ibid.

vii Weng, H. Y., Fox, A. S., Shackman, A. J., Stodola, D. E., Caldwell, J. Z., Olson, M. C., . . . Davidson, R. J. (2013). Compassion training alters altruism and neural responses to suffering. *Psychological Science, 24*(7), 1171–1180.

viii Lutz, A., Greischar, L. L., Rawlings, N. B., Ricard, M., & Davidson, R. J. (2004). Long-term meditators self-induce high-amplitude gamma synchrony during mental practice. *Proceedings of the National academy of Sciences of the United States of America, 101*(46), 16369–16373.

ix   Ibid.

x Breines, J. G., & Chen, S. (2012). Self-compassion increases self-improvement motivation. *Personality and Social Psychology Bulletin*, *38*(9), 1133–1143.

xi Ibid

xii Ibid

xiii Hạnh, N. (1990). Present moment, wonderful moment: Mindfulness verses for daily living (p. 3). Berkeley, CA: Parallax Press.

xiv See *Understanding Depression: A Harvard Medical School Special Health Report* (2013).

Acknowledgments

Everything I've learned about how to transform suffering and cultivate joy in myself and others, I have learned from Thich Nhat Hanh, the monks and nuns of Plum Village, and the other spiritual teachers I've been fortunate enough to meet. I can't thank them enough.

I also feel deep gratitude for the support and encouragement I've received from mentors and friends, especially Joanne Friday, Chris Germer, Richie Davidson, Dick Schwartz, Tara Brach, and Larry Boyang.

All of the people at W.W. Norton have been incredibly helpful in bringing this workbook into existence. Thanks so much for your guidance and believing in this project. Huge gratitude to Ben Yarling and Chuck Millar for your brilliant editing.

To my wonderful wife and son, Annie and Finnegan, thank you for being such an inspiration and source of love in the world.

Index

sending practice
   create your own phrases in, 102
   described, 99
   example of, 102
   instructions for, 100-1
   question related to, 102
sensitivity(ies)
   food, 134
shame
   erasing, 24-26
skill(s)
   self-compassion as, 13-16 *see also*
      self-compassion as skill
sleep
   in balanced lifestyle, 135-36
sleep deficiency
   CDC on, 135
   management of, 135
stories you are telling yourself
   self-acceptance practice for, 59
suffering
   embracing, 61-68 *see also* embracing
      suffering; embracing suffering practice
suffering in body
   listening to, 75, 77-79 *see also* listening
      to suffering in body practice
sugar
   in balanced lifestyle, 134
support
   community, 125

The Self-Compassion Skills Workbook,
   165
thought(s)
   conflicts in, 89
   mindfulness of *see* mindfulness of
      thoughts; mindfulness of thoughts
      practice
   types of, 58-59
   unrelated to emotion you're experienc-
      ing, 59
training sessions
   for self-compassion, ix-x
trauma
   healing from, 10

vegetable(s)
   in balanced lifestyle, 134
voice(s)
   healthy voice becoming kinder, 130-
      32
   kinder, 130-32
volunteering
   in balanced lifestyle, 136

well-being
   researchers who study, 109
when compassion is difficult practice,
   87-98 *see also* competing com-
      mitments as obstacle to self-
      compassion

About the Author

Tim Desmond is a practicing psychotherapist, author, and student of Zen Master Thich Nhat Hanh. Distinguished Faculty at Antioch University and co-founder of Morning Sun Mindfulness Center, he lives in Alstead, NH, and teaches mindfulness and self-compassion practices to professional and popular audiences all over the world. He has presented at hundreds of conferences, seminars, and universities, including Yale Medical School, the Psychotherapy Networker Symposium, and the Institute for Meditation and Psychotherapy, helping thousands of people discover the wisdom and powerful benefits of self-compassion. In addition to *The Self-Compassion Skills Workbook*, his publications include *Self-Compassion in Psychotherapy* (W. W. Norton, 2015).